A Survivor's Guide to Living in Ireland

Dedication

To all that dream of living in Ireland
and to the fervent wish that your dreams will come true
as mine have;

To Mary and Bill Richards,
parents and best friends;

To Kristin, Cathy & Jonathan,
the surprising results of a summer's cycling trip;

And to Bernadette,
My wild Irish Rose.

iii

A Survivor's Guide to Living in Ireland

Contents

Map of Ireland

Notes

If in a moment of uncertain insanity you have ever thought of abandoning the rat race by throwing an obnoxiously composed letter of resignation onto your boss's desk, then packing your spouse, children and dog into a forty-foot container and drifting across the sea to the green fields of Ireland for either a prolonged stay or the dream of actually living (and perhaps dying) in this far-flung location, then this book is for you.

A Survivor's Guide to Living in Ireland gives you the information to allow you to start the process of achieving that crazed dream. This book tells you how to: understand the often misunderstood Irish and the magical country within which they live; get a work permit; get a job; find a house; buy that house; understand the locals; fit in with the locals; educate your children; experience the wonder and mystery that is a pint of Guinness; and otherwise enjoy the exceptional experience of living in a country that is populated by a tapestry of people who are some of the most welcoming in the world.

This book is based on my personal experience of living for over twenty years in this country. Except for a very few creative and crazed liberties that I have taken, this is not a book of fiction: it is fact. It is not even a memoir but could possibly be described as one person's descent into insanity and the upward journey toward subsequent salvation. Whatever it is I hope that you'll find it useful.

While I have done my best to ensure that all figures and statistics mentioned in this small tome are accurate please don't take my word for it. Check things out for yourself. At the back, you'll find a series of references. Use them. Your local library is also a good place to start. I'll not have the fate of a would-be immigrant on my conscience particularly if you make the decision to move here based only on the ranting of this insane American expatriate.

I hope that you enjoy these few words as much as I enjoyed writing them. And I hope that they give you some idea of the magic – and occasional disaster – that can befall you should you choose to stay in this delightful country.

Tom Richards
Navan, County Meath, Ireland
August 2005

Prologue

Chicago, Illinois   *August 15, 1982*

Dear Tom,

Have you completely lost your mind? What ever possessed you to move to Ireland? You know what I taught you in history class. You will undoubtedly find the country and its people impossibly backward, impoverished and xenophobic.

Ireland is a tribal nation. As a complete outsider, you will undoubtedly be stabbed in the back at the first opportunity. I must say that I understand you even less than my son – and Robert has chosen to join the Peace Corps and has gone away to Peru of all places. I suspect that your parents are equally disturbed with your decision.

For Heaven's sake, grab that Irish wife of yours (another ill-made decision that I intend to discuss with you in the near future) and come back home immediately. You are wasting your life. Write back at once. You know how I worry.

Fondly,

Ronald

The above letter was received by me well over twenty years ago, penned by my old high school history teacher whom, as you can tell, was somewhat perturbed by a major decision that I had taken at the time.

The stream of events that Ronald alludes to can be summed up thusly:

In 1980 while on a bicycling holiday through England, I decided to make a left turn rather than a right at a particular crossroads in Wales. Had I turned right I would have continued through Wales, north to Scotland, back to London, and then caught the Freddie Laker flight home to San Francisco and to my waiting, if uncertain, fiancé. Inevitably, I would have followed the path of other young bucks my age: a career hell-bent on achieving vast sums of disposable income, a large house in some faceless American suburb, and a lifetime spent commuting on a mind-numbing freeway entombed in metal and plastic while listening to the *Eagles Greatest Hits* over and over again.

I don't think so.

Instead I turned left, which in turn led me to a small ferry port in Wales, which subsequently led me on to Ireland. I crossed the Irish Sea despite impending seasickness and finally docked in the small Irish port of Dun Laoghrie. From there, I cycled north to Dunleer in County Louth, and having been brought by fate to this lovely small village, met a beautiful woman whom I impetuously proposed to exactly three days later in a swimming pool surrounded by a group of innocent mentally handicapped Irish children. Though my parents, friends – and Ronald – thought that I should be immediately committed to the local asylum, and despite my wife's parents' feelings that this was some sort of fanciful summer romance soon to be forgotten, we were married the following December.

My Irish wife Bernadette, an absolutely stunning young blond with beautiful flashing green Irish eyes, had not thought-through what it might mean to be married to someone from a country vastly different from her own. Nor had I, come to think of it. I saw myself as her victorious American knight, and determined to take her home to the United States and away from the seeming backwardness of 1980's Ireland. The thought of setting up home in her country had never even crossed my mind. After all, why would I, a newly minted college post-graduate with a bright future before me, *ever* think of living in Ireland of all places? With my new bride at my side, we climbed onto an airplane bound for San Francisco and toward a life that could only come up roses.

As I said, I had not thought things through. In that I was only twenty-six at the time, however, I have long ago learned to forgive myself.

Eighteen months later my wife, having just given birth to our first daughter – and missing her Irish life to no small measure – decided that she was homesick and pleaded with me to take her home. As it happened, my bright future wasn't working out: I had just been given the sack by Avis Rent-A-Car. My uncaring boss

2

telephoned me in the hospital minutes after Bernie had given birth to Kristin and informed me that my job wasn't really all that important after all and would I kindly leave at the earliest convenience, which happened to be the next day.

We were already behind in our mortgage, America was in recession, and the prospects of finding another job seemed more than a little remote. After thinking it through for exactly one day (I was a little precocious back then) I made a decision.

We sold everything, loaded a couple of bags and our then three-month-old daughter on board a draughty charter jet and left for Ireland. Had I thought about it I possibly would have changed my mind. At that point in history the Irish were emigrating in droves the other way. It seemed that I was the only American – or other foreigner – crazy enough to think that I could possibly survive in Ireland. But I didn't think about it and one fine day found myself standing in Shannon Airport and quickly came to the realisation that perhaps I had indeed lost my mind.

I've been here ever since.

For over twenty-years, since July 1982, I have called Ireland – sometimes reverently, sometimes reluctantly – my home. Every now and then I get a phone call, letter, or email from a friend or colleague who is hell-bent either on immigrating here or coming for a prolonged stay. Each one, barely concealing their envy, asks me, "What's it like to live there?" And each one is surprised when I lay things on the table, bare my soul and crassly destroy the myths that they have of the place.

Ireland is not *The Quiet Man* let me tell you. At least not any more. When I tell them the reality of living here, I usually hear a static-filled pause as a lifetime of carefully constructed illusions are flushed down the toilet. It usually goes something like this:

> *Friend* (in alarm): 'You mean that everyone has a car now?'
> *Me* (trying to be patient): 'That's right. Sometimes two. Maybe even three.'
> *Friend*: 'Three cars? But what about the donkey carts? The ones on all of the tourist brochures?'
> *Me* (getting more frustrated): 'The carts were burned when they put in the new motorways, right after the government bought all of the farmland in a compulsory

3

> order, and for all I know the donkeys are now retired and living a life of luxury in Majorca.'
> *Friend*: 'But that's horrible! Ireland is supposed to be so quaint!'

'Quaint'. Now there is a word that I have come to absolutely abhor. Years ago I also believed that Ireland was quaint. But let me tell you something: Ireland has changed. Today, it is a sophisticated, growing, European country populated by some wonderful, if at times rather obstreperous, people. Yet so many of the world's citizens, especially the Irish, try to deny that fact.

But when I try to explain this new mind-set to my friends they usually think that I'm either still insane or am living in some sort of isolated monastery and don't really have the right to an opinion on the matter.

Having been asked so many times what it's like to live here and what it's been like to survive twenty years and more of Ireland I finally decided that it was high time that I put down on paper what little I know about this country and its people. If nothing else it will save me the bother of having to rewrite it every time I get a phone call from some long-lost friend asking me to tell them how to move here, how to get a job, what to bring, what not to bring, what to expect, where to go, and what to see when they get over here.

And of course I won't have to expand on what it's 'like' anymore. I'll start thusly, and remove immediately some of the most popular misconceptions of this country. To whit:

After half a lifetime of mishaps, mistakes, mad escapes, conversations both riveting and infinitely boring, hope-filled wanderings through potholes both large and small, contemplative walks through misty rains, wild dashes through thunderous downpours, and careful – sometimes drunken – philosophical observations of both this country and its citizenry, I start by imparting some riveting knowledge of what Ireland *isn't*.

Ireland *isn't* a part of the United Kingdom (suggest that to an Irishman and you'll find a balled up fist under your gob), nor is it a country of federal democracy such as the United States (it is ruled by a parliamentary democracy modelled on the United Kingdom). Ireland is no longer an agricultural society, although a significant portion of its exports are still agricultural-based. It is not a twee mystical world full of little people or faeries, pushbike riding businessmen, or horse-pulled trams.

Ireland is absolutely *not* a country devoid of trees, Coca-Cola, personal computers, hotdogs, pizza, coffee, fast freeways, international airports, digital telephones, hot water, indoor toilets, cell phones, big screen plasma televisions, central heating systems, dishwashers, exterior and interior house paint that comes in colours other than white, tile roofed houses rather than falling-down shanties wearing thatch caps, fancy cars owned by most of the populace, Personal Digital Assistants, iPods, out of wedlock childbirth, divorce, black people, brown people, Asians, Africans, Americans, Italians, French, Germans, Poles, Russians and other peoples of the world, decaffeinated tea and coffee, low fat milk, or any of a thousand things and peoples that my friends, in their unfortunate ignorance, believe to be central to the character of this country. Mind you, when I first moved here in 1982 many of the material items mentioned above were decidedly absent.

No one says 'Top of the morning to you!' on a cold and blustery autumn morning. Thatch cottages, except for an occasional bed & breakfast or as part of a tourist trap, have made way for two-storied red-tiled suburban housing. And the people, though still some of the most welcoming in the world, have begun to develop the cynical attitudes present in America, England, and much of the rest of the West. If you think that Ireland is still a land of milk, honey, and the occasional leprechaun, you'll have a hard time surviving here.

So what is Ireland, then, exactly? Well, that's a good question. It's what I'm always asked, come to think of it. And I've never been able to properly answer in a sentence or two. The Ireland of today is much different from that of 1982. In the intervening years, I have watched as Ireland has attempted – sometimes successfully, sometimes not – to become part of the modern world.

Liken it to a tapestry still in construction: a wonderful fabric woven together with small 'quaint' villages clogged with modern traffic; folklore and mystical tales cobbled next to twenty-first century technology; miles of country lanes still sporting large potholes that can swallow entire cars; crazed drivers that don't yet understand how to navigate traffic congestion; stupendous sunsets that have not yet surrendered to Western pollution; maddening weather that everyone still talks about despite everything; cruel taxation that the government says is getting easier to swallow – but none of us believe anything that the government says. And, of course, the best pint of beer this side of heaven.

Ireland is an anomaly. It is a quickly changing society that is trying to drag itself into the new millennium, with much gnashing of teeth in the process. If you are planning to venture out this way for whatever reason – on vacation, as part of a work assignment, or pursuing a personal dream of permanently settling here – you had best be prepared for the challenge. Maybe I can help.

I've survived in this country for over twenty years. And if I can do it, so can you.

Guideline One
Don't Believe Anything You Have Read, It Probably Isn't True

Chicago, Illinois   *May 1, 1980*

My Dear Tom,

I am absolutely delighted to have received your letter. Your decision to take a short vacation to Ireland is absolutely correct, particularly after the rigors of graduate school. You will find the charm of its ancient people warm and invigorating, if somewhat pre-modern.

I am certain that you will love the country and its history. That said, avoid Northern Ireland at all costs in that you will undoubtedly be shot as a gunrunner.

As you know, Ireland has no trees. These were borne off by the English when constructing their great fleet in defence of the Spanish. Nor will you find indoor plumbing other than in the largest cities, telephones that work except in government buildings, or adequate heating systems except in the Ambassador's residence. Do make certain to bring along your woollies.

It has been over fifteen years since I last trod the broken roads of the Irish countryside during a sabbatical to that far-off land and I suspect that nothing has changed. Nor is it likely to, at least not in our lifetimes.

Fondly,

Ronald

I should perhaps explain that I have no Irish blood whatsoever running through my veins. My ancestry positively excludes Ireland but is instead littered with a hodgepodge of other immigrant nations who made their way to North America and the United States in hopes of finding a better life.

French Acadian, Dutch, German and English genes have undoubtedly managed to screw up my DNA makeup to no end. Rumour has it that we even have a little Native American kicking around in us somewhere. Along the line we picked up some Scottish blood, which perhaps gives me some sort of predisposition toward the Celts. Maybe that was the genetic magnet that called me toward Ireland. But I don't think so. The warring factions in my genes, even without the benefit of Irish-ness, have in all likelihood made me crazy enough to consider just about anything.

The Richards' on my father's father's side, the Buote's on my father's mother's side, the Pethtel's on my mother's father's side, and the Scott's on my mother's mother's side, were solidly American. Some first settled in Prince Edward Island way up in the Northeast corner of Canada and then, having been kicked out by the English, moved to wild outposts around Boston. Others purportedly came over on the Mayflower and took up residency, eventually fighting the British in the Revolutionary War, then each other in the Civil War.

My kin helped to settle the Ohio Valley, fought in World War I, World War II, Korea and Vietnam. Way back when they were honest-to-God pioneers. My ancestors loved America to bits. They really enjoyed packing into some Godforsaken corner of the world and hacking out a little place in the wilderness in which to call home. Growing up in the 1950's, '60's, and '70's as I did, all of the wilderness in America had already been overrun by fast food joints, strip malls and super highways. Though I never intended to be a pioneer, perhaps my genes insisted that I should locate a new wilderness in which to make my mark. A place to chop down a tree or boil the locals in oil, something like that.

So God only knows what my ancestors would have thought of their great-great-great-great grandson who decided to turn his back on all of their hard work and head east rather than west. I've probably made them turn in their graves.

My point is that nothing prepared me for, nor gave me cause to consider, a lifetime of living in Ireland. Perhaps the genetic need to roam the world and conquer other lands is still buried somewhere deep inside me. I'm not sure. What I do know is that when I finally decided to come to this ancient land of saints and scholars I was completely unprepared for the experience. I was naïve, uncertain, unaware, and believed everything that I had ever read or heard about the country, which to be frank wasn't much.

Big mistake.

Most Americans – and may I say, peoples from many other nations even if they make a blood claim to Irish ancestry – seem to possess no sense of Irish history whatsoever. I admit a similar ignorance though perhaps I have some excuse in that having no Irish heritage I was totally unaware of things Irish. What I knew about Ireland was gleaned from watching John Ford's classic film *The Quiet Man* every St Patrick's Day – not quite the education one would seem to require if intending to blend in with the locals. I did attend Catholic school when I was eight, and Sister Raymond Francis taught us to sing 'When You're Irish, Come Into the Parlour', but that was about it.

Prior to coming here I thought the entire country was full of peace-loving people who had spent the past three thousand years growing turnips and potatoes, and who occasionally took out their frustrations at not having won the hand of the local beauty by beating each other senseless. Then I discovered that the potato didn't arrive in Ireland until the 16th Century, a piece of information that continues to baffle me.

Therefore, and assuming that many others desire to up-end their lives by moving to or visiting this part of the world, perhaps it is best to start with a short discussion of the history of this small island. Ireland, as it turns out, has a wonderfully colourful – if bloody – history that should have given me some sort of warning of what to expect when moving here.

The world has known about this country since people first started writing things and creating maps. The Greeks were the first to mention Ireland in an obscure text by Festus Rufus Avienus, based on another text (plagiarising began early it seems) with its origins in the sixth century B.C. Ptolemy, the map-maker and geographer, even illustrated a pretty good likeness of the island in the form of a cubist-looking map dating from seventy A.D. or so. It is so bizarre looking that Picasso possibly used it for inspiration.

What with a map on how to get here, Irish tourism of the bloody kind began fairly early.

Ireland has always been invaded by races both mythical and factual – Nemedians, Fir Bolg, Tuatha De Danann – but at some point or other the pre-historic Irish were conquered by the Celts and that's when all the trouble started. From that point it seems that every country with a bloodthirsty army to support it had designs on Ireland. They either wanted to trade with it or conquer it. Even back when people ran around in small boats and waved short swords at each other everyone wanted a piece of the small little country shaped somewhat like a mystical Teddy bear.

The Romans didn't bother conquering the country – they considered it the End of the World, and besides they had enough trouble trying to keep the warring English tribes under their thumb. They did, however, do a little trading with Ireland, which managed to keep everyone happy.

As the Roman Empire started to fall apart Roman rule in England went to hell and some of the Irish kings got together and decided that England – just over the other side of the Irish Sea – would be a perfect spot for a little rape, pillaging, and kidnapping. So that's exactly what they did. I doubt that the Irish raiders made many good friends in England, and when the tables were turned and the English invaded Ireland I suspect that every John Bull decided that it was high time to get his own back.

One of the many people the Irish brought back in chains was the man who later went on to become Ireland's patron saint: the Welshman – of Roman extraction – known as Patricius, or Saint Patrick to you and me. Life in Ireland became even more stressful with the coming of this saintly man. In my opinion, Patrick (God bless him) did more to ruin Ireland than any throng of invading Viking hoards. He not only brought Christianity to Ireland but also paved the way for the establishment of the Catholic Church (not the Roman Catholic variety, however, in that this particular brand of Catholicism had not yet been invented). The Church was hot into property acquisition in those days and one of the first things that they did was to divide up the country for themselves. The Irish Kings, thinking that they were in danger of being damned for all time (and perhaps being condemned to a hell even worse than the miserable Ireland of the first century in which they lived) played along.

The result was that the Catholic aristocracy kept a tight grip on the entire populace of this country. The Irish have trembled in their boots, bowing before any cleric that looks strangely at them, right up to the last twenty years or so. I shouldn't, of course, be too unkind or snivelling regarding the Catholic invasion. The teachings of the Church and its priests and monks did, after all, help to preserve small things like the written word and basic education. If it hadn't been for them all of Europe (and the rest of the world, perhaps) might have devolved into savages with the coming of the Dark Ages. It seems that the light of knowledge was kept aflame in this out-of-the-way corner of the world, making Ireland briefly The Land of Saints and Scholars. Eventually, the Irish priests let the word out and helped to fan this tiny spark of Irish custodianship into a first class Renaissance.

That said, the Church also managed to inflict a great deal of damage on the Irish population including rape, fraud, collusion with the enemy, and a general feeling of insecurity and harsh feeling. You might not guess it but many Irish are fundamentally guilt ridden and insecure. Over a thousand years of iron-fisted Church rule does that to a civilisation, doesn't it? I've often wondered what would have happened if Patrick had been executed at a stake by some ill-mannered pagan Irish King who thought Christianity to be nonsense. We could, of course, now be communicating by heathen drumbeats but I suspect that the Irish might be a little happier all the same.

Then the Vikings blew through in the seventh century and set up camp for a while. They built a few things along the River Liffey in what is now Dublin, and have since provided occasional excitement in that every time the Dublin County Council digs a new channel for gasworks they uncover a Viking wall or whorehouse, and the archaeologists run down with shovels and brushes in hand and for a while the locals become happily involved in a great deal of historically interesting work. The Vikings also promoted that wonderful economic activity called slavery, in addition to a little coinage and beer making, and for some time things must have been pretty lively in the country. Little did the Irish know that they too would soon face several hundred years of servitude.

In the middle of all of this, Irish kings kept running their own small feudal principalities with some little success. It seems that they took out most of their frustration at being conquered all of the time by attacking each other, which makes perfect sense.

Maybe that's where Irish begrudgery got its start. If a relative, friend, or the King next door had grown above his station the local neighbours started saying that he was a twit. Soon everyone recognised this fact, and so a fellow who might be completely innocent of anything could suddenly find that everyone in town hated his guts and would begin throwing verbal abuse. The other option, of course, was to attack him with a vast army and stab him with a short sword.

The fact that Ireland was next conquered by a mean-spirited group of English tyrants also has something to do with the country's general psychoses. In 1175, an Irish twit by the name of Dermot MacMurrogh, the King of Leinster, was kicked out of his kingdom. To get even he asked England's King Henry II for some help. Henry decided to recruit some Norman knights for a little adventure and the result was the establishment of an English beachhead in Ireland.

Thereafter, and for a few hundred years, it's back and forth as the Irish try to get the upper hand on the English and vice-versa. During that period, the English did what they could to drive home Anglo rule including the declaration that all of Ireland was a mere province of a new English empire. Needless to say, many Irish didn't like the idea and the short wars got only worse.

However, in 1649 an English fellow by the name of Cromwell decided that he'd had enough and decided to pay a little visit himself. He also brought along a vast armed force complete with sharp swords and a thirst for Irish blood. The Irish didn't stand a chance. The result was almost complete English domination for the next four hundred years or so.

The lot of the Irish was made even more difficult when, in the mid-eighteen hundreds, a farmer suddenly realised that his entire potato crop looked more than a little constipated. He sent out a general alarm but it was too late. The potato blight had hit and what seemed to be every potato in Ireland was lost. The fact that the Irish depended on the lowly potato for most of their nutritional needs meant that Irish folks died in droves.

At the start of the blight, over eight million people called this wee island their home. A few years later, following starvation, death, and immigration, only three million souls remained. So if when travelling through Ireland you see a ramshackle, deserted, falling down shanty, it could well be the ancient home of a family who died of the Hunger or chucked it all in for a new start in America or Australia. Chances are that they never survived the trip. When you see those old falling down walls, say a prayer. Those long-ago occupants might need it still.

England, their foreign masters, hardly did anything to help the fate of their Irish subjects. While it is true that some of the local landlords really did their best to help the Irish keep body and soul together, their rulers across the Irish Sea did little except to set up a few workhouses to call home. For the next seventy years or so Ireland and its people suffered.

By 1916, the Irish had had enough. A group of seeming madmen, armed with little more than conviction and a love for liberty, decided that the English should be booted across the Irish Sea and back to England where they belonged. On Easter Monday of that year (24 April, 1916 to be exact), all hell broke loose. The heroes of Ireland – including Pearse, Connolly, and assorted brave hearts – occupied the General Post Office in Dublin, attempting to keep from getting killed while the English threw everything they had at them. These valiant Irishmen held out long enough to distribute their proclamation of freedom within the capital city, a proclamation that reads thusly:

Poblacht na hEireann
The Provisional Government of the Irish Republic

"To the People of Ireland ....."

Irishmen and Irishwomen! In the name of God and of the dead generations from which she receives the old tradition of nationhood, Ireland, through us, summons her children to her flag, and strikes for her freedom ....

We declare the right of the people of Ireland to the ownership of Ireland, and to the unfettered control of Irish destinies, to be sovereign and indefeasible......In every generation the Irish people have asserted their right to National freedom and sovereignty; six times during the past three hundred years they have asserted it in arms. Standing on that fundamental right and again asserting it in arms in the face of the world, we hereby proclaim the Irish Republic as a Sovereign Independent Sate, and we pledge our lives and the lives of our comrades to the cause of its freedom, of its welfare, and of its exaltation among the nations ......

The Republic guarantees civil and religious liberty, equal rights and equal opportunities to all its citizens, and declares its resolve to pursue the happiness and prosperity of the whole nation and of all its parts, cherishing all the children of the nation equally, and oblivious of the differences carefully fostered by an alien government, which have divided a minority from the majority in the past ......

We place the cause of the Irish Republic under the protection of the Most High God, whose blessing we invoke upon our arms...... In this supreme hour the Irish nation must, by its valour and discipline, and by the readiness of its children, to sacrifice themselves for the common good, prove itself worthy of the august destiny to which it is called.

Signed on behalf of the Provisional Government

Thomas J Clarke
Sean MacDiarmada
Thomas MacDonagh
P H Pearse
Eamon Ceannt
James Connolly
Joseph Plunkett

Unfortunately, these brave men were later captured and all shot by the British. But their sacrifice got the ball of independence rolling.

After a great deal of negotiation on both sides, things finally changed when in 1922 the Irish finally got their act together with the formation of a provisional independent Irish government. After a great deal of acrimony between the Irish and English, together with an Irish Civil War and the exclusion of Ulster from the newly formed Irish Republic (an entire quarter of the Island of Ireland as it turns out), everyone seemed to have calmed down for a time. That said, and even today, is it any wonder that a few English people may occasionally be reviled with the polite phrase 'You English bastard!' by some Irish fool? This makes it perfectly clear why some English visitors who are brave enough to walk into a local tavern drink their pints in such a nervous fashion.

The Irish, it seems, have long memories. Based on their unfortunate history you can't really blame them. It also goes a long way to explaining why some Irish men, fuelled to the gills with drink, prefer to end heated discussions with fists rather than a reasonable vocal response.

Recently, however, things have started to get better. A 'Peace Process' began in earnest in the mid-1990's. Now the English and the Irish, while they might still stare suspiciously at each other, will at least shake hands before starting to yell names and often get along tolerably well.

But despite this progress, many of my American and European friends have not yet heard of this astonishing outcome. When visiting the bright lights of New York or the busy streets of London I'm often asked if the Troubles are still as lively as they were heretofore. Without a doubt, the answer is a resounding 'No!' But even back in the '80's, when the Troubles were at their height, Ireland was safer than often depicted in the world's press. Living north of Dublin as I do, and in the geographic corridor that has often been associated with the IRA and their doubtful campaign of hatemongering, I can assure you that my family and I were never in any danger. We were never accosted by any IRA hooligans. We never heard the bang of loud explosives (until recently, that is, when the film *Omagh*, depicting the Real IRA's bombing of that Northern Ireland town that resulted in so many deaths, was shot in Navan. On that occasion, what seemed to be the entire population trooped down to watch as the film's Special Effects people turned one of the town's main streets into a land of carnage.) In fact, throughout the years of my stay here, we have been as safe as houses.

Yet the perception among many of the world's populace is that murder and mayhem continue to terrify and disrupt Ireland's citizenry, both North and South of the boarder. While it is true that the Peace Process has not yet been entirely finalised, it is also true that Ireland's politicians are working frantically to ensure that the current peace will be maintained. If you are still in doubt about your safety here you'll just have to take my word for it: you're safer on Belfast's city streets at midnight than you would be on certain Los Angeles thoroughfares at high noon.

The majority of the citizens of Ireland – Catholic, Protestant, Unionist and Nationalist – have finally taken a common stand. Except for a handful of thugs from all sides that refuse to accept change, most people here of all persuasions agree that the time for killing is at an end. After hundreds of years of religious and politically motivated bloodshed, the Irish have almost reached a lasting peace. For that, all parties involved should be truly proud.

Living here has allowed me to immerse myself in the history and culture of this people. But before I moved here permanently I hadn't bothered to learn much, if anything, about Irish history. In fact, I didn't know too much about the place at all except what I had gleaned from the afore-mentioned *Quiet Man* film, numerous travel brochures, and the rebel lyrics of songs sung by the Clancy Brothers.

In any event, and despite my ancestral predisposition to conquer new lands, and even if I had gone to the bother of reading a complete unadulterated history of the country, I was doomed to learn how to survive in Ireland the hard way.

A Survivor's Guide to Living in Ireland

Guideline Two
How to Get a Job and Also Survive

Chicago, Illinois   *November 16, 1982*

Dear Tom,

I was stung by your most recent letter of the 1st of the month stating that you have decided to stay in that foreign country. I find it impossible to believe that you are bull-headed enough to continue living there while still being out of work! Undoubtedly, you will find it next to impossible to obtain gainful employment in that land of poverty. When are you going to come to your senses and realize that your future is much more important than your dreams of destitution?

Please write back at once. If you need airfare for the trip home, I am more than willing to help in that I am certain that your parents are no longer talking to you.

Ronald

When I breezed into the country back in '82, wife and child in hand, I thought that getting a job would be easy. Why wouldn't it? I was qualified, wasn't I? I had experience. After all, I had an MBA from UCLA hadn't I? My enthusiasm was matched only by my ignorance.

In 1982 Ireland was embroiled in one of the worst recessions in its history. It seemed that for the past few years the Irish government had decided to spend well beyond its means, attempting to drag itself into the twentieth century by funding massive construction (much of it borrowed from a number of International Financial Institutions) that it could little afford. To pay-off the borrowings it raised taxes. This had the effect of creating inflation, higher interest rates, and a skyrocketing unemployment rate that quickly approached twenty percent of the working population. While new roads were being built, the economy of the nation was being ground into wholemeal. Interest rates reached fifteen percent and more. Ireland was on its knees.

Despite this, and with his eyes wide shut, this young American confidently stepped into the breach of immigration not knowing what was about to hit him.

For the next three months, and without a job or the prospect of same, I carefully studied the local want ads, sending out enthusiastic missives, expectantly waiting for those cheerful responses that would inevitably lead to an interview and subsequent employment.

My wait was in vain. For you see, most Irish companies didn't answer letters from those seeking employment. I've never understood the reason why. Perhaps it's because the Human Resource people were busy drinking down in the local pub or were trying to pick the next winner at the Cheltenham Races. What I am now certain of, however, is that all of my letters ended up in the bin next to remnants of cold coffee and cigarette ends.

Consequently, I took to the streets. I plodded the main office blocks, knocking on doors in a futile attempt to ingratiate myself with the local business intelligencia. Unfortunately, I never made it past the reception desk. Most of the sweet young receptionists that I met took one look at me, nodded agreeably at my verbal waffle, and told me that the boss was unavailable. Though I left numerous resumes along my journey no one – not one – responded.

Next I tried the telephone but with the same results. No one wanted to talk to me. In fact, rather than an interview, they suggested that I post in my details but I already knew that my well-crafted letters would head toward the first available bin and sure oblivion.

Then one night in the local pub, with my meagre financial resources running out and my emotional mindset contemplating suicide, I sat literally crying into my drink and mentioned my plight to a local. And that's how I discovered the secret of getting a job in Ireland.

Networking.

We all know the importance of networking when it comes to getting a job. We've long been taught that who we know is much more important than what we know. But nowhere is this simple premise more important than in Ireland.

For you see, Ireland is a village. The twenty-six counties within the Republic of Ireland contain a mere 3.8 million souls, or so said the most recent government census. Add to that another 1 million living in the six counties of Northern Ireland and you can see that all of Ireland could be housed easily enough within the San Francisco Bay Area.

But the small population alone does not in and of itself give credence to networking. Other factors are at work here, one of the most important being the art of conversation. The Irish love to talk and they'll talk about almost anything: the state of Irish politics, the weather (a constant source of verbal acrobatics), their neighbours and relatives, the colour of their living room wallpaper, the antics that they got up to on their most recent holiday abroad...the list goes on and on.

This propensity to chat is reinforced by an incredible supply of information sources, a list that I suspect would be envied by some of my fellow Americans living in their reinforced continent. The Irish, a highly intelligent lot, are voracious consumers of news and considering the size of their population they have a whole lot to choose from. The Republic alone supports three national daily newspapers, not to mention assorted Sunday papers, as well as countless tabloids and English broadsheets. Any community of ten thousand or so also has a local newspaper.

This deluge of written words is supplemented by cable television. While the Irish do not enjoy the thousands of television channels available to many American or European citizens (most of which contain a dross of suspect, so-called entertainment), the Irish do have access to any number of news channels including the national stations (RTE, RTE Two, and TV Three), English stations (BBC, ITV, Channel Four, Sky), a number of American channels (CNN, CNBC, Fox), a wide range of other international news carriers (including but not limited to Euro News, CCTV – the China news channel, and Vectone World), as well as a couple of Arabic television stations.

This stunning range of news coverage is supplemented by a number of 'foreign' language stations (broadcast in languages other than English). So if a viewer happens to be competent in Spanish, French or German, and has nothing else to do, he or she could be quite content to spend an entire week catching up on those events that make the world go round. The result is that the Irish can obtain any number of competing viewpoints that provide fuel to the fires of communication.

This characteristic – this gift of the gab – means that a verbal account of almost anything can be spread like wildfire, should it be properly kindled and fanned. This gift has been handed down from generation to generation, and most probably emanates from the *Seaneachi* (the ancient Irish for Storyteller) from long ago.

Properly utilised, this propensity to talk about almost anything can be used to land a job.

In my case, and with time running out, my drinking partner suggested that I talk to one of his relatives. He, in turn, chatted to a neighbour regarding the poor unfortunate who was so constrained by lack of money that his child was being forced to eat yesterday's boiled potatoes.

The neighbour talked to a distant friend who owned an electrical components supplier and who was fortunate enough to be occasionally hired by an electrical weighing systems company. The components supplier, in turn, talked to the managing director of the weighing company (who was a good friend of his) and a week later I was hired as a salesman responsible for travelling the width and breadth of Ireland to twist the arms of local farmers into purchasing expensive cattle weighing systems.

Networking in Ireland can pay off and it continues to do so even with the advent (and possible demise) of the so-called Celtic Tiger. The Irish economy of the new millennium has been one of staggering growth and a magnet for billions of dollars in inward investment. Companies such as Microsoft, Intel, IBM, Google, Dell, Yahoo and many, many others have now established operations in the country, using Ireland to access the rest of the world's markets, as a location for a variety of tax incentives, and as a resource renowned for its highly educated workforce.

During this period of exponential economic growth (approximately 1996 through 2001), getting a job was as easy as downing a pint of Guinness and many of the methods that citizens of other nations are familiar with often yielded quick results. Employment agencies and executive search firms came into their own. Companies would return calls. Internet employment search sites began to blossom. Everyone was having a grand old time.

More recently, however, and with the bursting of the Internet bubble, Ireland has begun to suffer along with every other world economy. At the time of this writing things are somewhat tougher than heretofore. Having grown at a double-digit pace since the mid-1990's the Irish economy is settling into a pattern of more sustainable, single-figure growth rates. Though it is somewhat more difficult to get a job than it was before, most people who really desire employment are able to find it.

That said, newly emerging patterns of immigration are having an impact on the Irish job scene. Recently, the European Union (of which Ireland is a part) grew by another ten countries. Total EU membership now stands at twenty-five nations, with an additional four countries having applied for membership. Citizens of the European Union have the right to work anywhere within the EU. And many of them – particularly from Eastern European countries such as Poland, Hungary and Slovenia, as well as citizens of non-EU nations including Russia, Nigeria, and other African countries – are voting with their feet and moving to Ireland in record numbers. All of them hope to grab a little part of the Irish economic miracle for themselves.

The government, now concerned about the possible political fall-out from uncontrolled immigration, has started to turn the screws. For years, Ireland was a country of net emigration. Now it is a country that acts as an economic magnet for the world's population, including the disenfranchised. And all of these people want a job. The Irish, having never dreamed that their country would attract so much interest from would-be international job seekers, have started to scream in protest. A minority actually believe that these people are going to rob this little corner of the world of opportunity, and believe that wholesale immigration must be restrained, and preferably stopped altogether. In response, the government has taken the stance of making it as difficult as possible for non-EU immigrants to gain entry to the country.

So what does this mean if you, dear reader, are hoping to hop aboard a draughty charter jet in search of a new life in the wilds of Ireland? It means that you again have to use tried and trusted networking methods. But before you start drafting your resume, there's more that you should understand.

A Survivor's Guide to Living in Ireland

First, and unless you are an EU national, or are married to an Irish or European Union citizen, your chances of getting a job and remaining in the country are limited. If you are married to an Irish or European national, you are automatically entitled to the right to work here. You are even entitled to apply for your Irish citizenship after a few years of residency.

You are also automatically entitled to Irish citizenship if one of your parents is Irish, or if your grandparents were Irish and registered the birth of your parent with the Irish government. In such cases you are automatically entitled not only to live and work here but also to obtain a European Union passport.

If you are American and choose to take up Irish citizenship you will not, fortunately, have to turn your back on the United States. The State Department has changed its rules and now you are more than welcome to carry both passports.

If however, like many, you do not have a recent Irish ancestor at your disposal or can not find a potential Irish bride or groom that turns your head enough to take that long walk down the church aisle, your journey will be more difficult though by no means impossible.

To get a job here you will require a work permit. The rules in this area are rather convoluted but the key point is this: you can only get a work permit by selling yourself to an employer who can't find anyone else in the country with particular skill-sets. Certain skills including IT professionals, nurses, doctors, and medical staff, continue to be in high demand. Ireland can't seem to get enough of them. Other professional areas in which you might have specific skill-sets – including banking, finance, and certain design skills – are also in short supply. These industries welcome foreign nationals with open arms because the local population simply can't meet the demand for these specialist skill-sets.

So, acquiring a permit now becomes a two-stage process: first, you have to find an employer with a job whose skills are in short supply. Second, you must convince that employer that you are worthy enough to have him or her go through the hassle of getting you that work permit, a permit that costs that employer some five hundred euro a year and which must be paid if he or she is to legally employ you.

Also, and even with a work permit, you'll have to 'register' every few months with the local police. When coming here, and even though I was married to an Irish national, I had to go through this same process until I was eventually 'officially' registered. And even after that – and for the next fifteen years until I bothered to apply for my Irish citizenship – I had that wonderful pleasure of walking down to the local police station (known in the Irish as the Garda Siochana, and a great group of guys and gals they are too) to register with the Force and let them know that I hadn't yet knocked off the local bank or mugged a little old lady for the contents of her handbag.

As a newly arrived immigrant where do you start to look for a job and that elusive work permit? You could, of course, start by running through the newspapers, walking the streets, or standing on top of a building and begging all and sundry for a job. But I don't think that you'll find those methods very effective.

As already mentioned, the best way of getting a job in Ireland is through networking of course. Even if you're new here and recently off the boat or aircraft, I can safely advise you that networking in Ireland is easy to do. Visit the local pub. Strike up a conversation. Tell people – beg people – to give you a hand...that you're a poor newly arrived immigrant who loves the country with a passion, who longs to live here. And that you could really use some advice and some contacts.

Then keep at it. Follow leads. Use the phone. In fact, buy a mobile phone. Everyone uses them and though the Irish pay higher cell phone rates than almost anyone in Europe it's still a great resource and allows prospective employers to easily get in touch with you. The Irish are also mad into using their mobile phones to text each other. Some of the younger citizens of this country can text messages faster than a speeding bullet. Texting is also much less expensive than voice – but whatever you do, make certain that people can contact you.

Then enhance your resume (called a Curriculum Vitae or CV over here) illustrating not only your past experience but how your skills can fit into niche areas that are in demand.

Emphasise energy and commitment. It's no secret that Ireland sells itself on its young, vibrant, well-educated workforce. If you, like me, are past your mid-thirties, you'll find it tougher to get a job. But be persistent. Understand that in many ways Ireland is still finding itself. It is still developing its skill-sets. You, as a person from another country, possibly possess skills not available here. If you're American or from a larger European nation then you possibly have experience working in huge, sophisticated markets. To survive in those economies, companies and their personnel must develop capabilities to flourish despite stiff competition. If you have such experience and skills – and if you spend some time to see how you can apply that experience to this market – you can make a difference over here particularly if you can provide businesses with export assistance and advice (the Irish economy is a net exporter which always results in an astoundingly positive national balance of payments). Communicate your skills base correctly and you can prove that you have much to offer.

Having found that employment opportunity, bug the hell out of the employer to get that work permit. As mentioned, it will cost your future employer not only time but also money to employ you, so (nicely) beleaguer the poor person with stories of your experience, intelligence, and willingness to work.

And finally, if all else fails, consider establishing a business here (see the Chapter below about possible opportunities). Potential immigrants who set up their own businesses and who create jobs – and subsequent taxes – for the Irish economy are entitled to apply for their own work permit and have little difficulty in obtaining one. Though Ireland is small it is a land of opportunity. Small and medium-sized businesses, as with the United States, England, Australia, and throughout the EU, have been the engine that has driven economic growth in this country.

If you have an idea, go for it. Having become your own boss in what is now a land of entrepreneurs, you'll never again have to go looking for permission to work or stay here.

And then, of course, you pay tax.

Having landed a job, you will – naturally enough – look forward to your first paycheque. If you're working for a company, you will quickly discover the absolute horrors that many of us go through when payday finally rolls around. In short, prepare yourself to be staggered by the amount of tax that you're going to pay to the government for the simple pleasure of working for a living.

Money Magazine recently conducted a survey of taxation levels within all EU countries. Their 'tax pain barometer' noted that, despite contrary opinion, Irish citizens do not carry the highest level of taxation burden in Europe. That dubious honour goes to the citizens of France. But taxation in Ireland is mighty high, let me tell you.

The Irish government does its best to tax almost everything in sight. Employees pay two types of tax: PAYE (Pay As You Earn, which is somewhat like the U.S. government's IRS Income Tax) and PRSI (Pay Related Social Insurance, akin to U.S. Social Security).

For most employees, PAYE starts out at twenty percent, jumping almost instantly to forty two percent. PRSI is an additional six percent or so. Your employer also has to pay an extra 10.75 percent in PRSI on top of employee contributions.

For this dubious pleasure, workers receive modest unemployment assistance should times get tough plus a childcare allowance (based on the number of children that you have in your family) each month even when working. When we all reach 65, we also receive a miserly government pension plus – and get this – a bus pass that allows us to travel on any public bus for free. Isn't that wonderful?

But the government also rips off Irish consumers with any number of 'stealth' taxes. We have a sales tax here with the inept title of 'Value Added Tax' or VAT. How it adds value is beyond me. Almost everything that a person purchases in this country automatically attracts a tax of twenty-one percent. So if you buy a can of Coke for one euro, the government will receive twenty one percent (or 17.35 cent) of the purchase price.

VAT is applied to almost anything that you can imagine: shoes, men's suit coats, Christmas decorations, toilet paper, babies' nappies, bottled water, alcohol…you get the idea. To my knowledge the only items that are exempt from VAT are certain food items, postage (we already pay high enough postage rates anyway) and, thanks be to God, books.

But the government's take doesn't end there. If you buy a television, not only do you pay VAT on the purchase price but you are also obliged to purchase a wonderful little document called a Television Licence.

A Survivor's Guide to Living in Ireland

What, you might ask, is a Television Licence? This wonderful piece of paper, required by all of us who possess a television, is a great example of the type of creativity that the government employs to rip off the Irish taxpayer. While it is called a licence it is actually a tax on those invisible signals that fly through the misty skies all by themselves, and if you own a TV and don't buy a Television Licence you can be prosecuted and handed a stiff fine of six hundred and thirty four euro.

You are legally obligated to buy such a licence each and every year if you have a television in your place of residence or at the job, and whether it is in working order or not. Technically, you are also obliged to buy a licence for each and every television and television receiver that you own (including any that might be incorporated into your computer, for instance). But most Irish draw the line at purchasing more than one hellaciously expensive licence and do their best to avoid paying for more.

The annual fee for this document is currently one hundred and fifty two euro, but don't worry, it's bound to go up.

What makes this fee even more galling is the fact that all funds collected in this manner go directly to that wonderful local publicly funded television station, Radio Telefis Eireann (RTE). With these moneys RTE is supposed to finance the production of well-crafted and entertaining programming. Unfortunately, and for years, RTE has been the butt of constant jokes. RTE is renowned throughout the country for producing some of the worst television drama in Europe. Such mind-numbing programmes as *Fair City* (a soap in which both scripts and actors seem to have a perpetual case of rigor-mortis) and the delightful game show *Tele-Bingo* (an absolutely inane programme premised on the stunning idea of broadcasting Bingo to the people of the country) cause one to wonder why producers have been employed for large money in that any six-year-old could surely come up with more interesting premises. To be fair, RTE does produce good (though sometimes biased) news programming, some great documentaries, and the occasional batch of wildly entertaining sports coverage. But if you're looking for pure entertainment you'd best give RTE a miss and go directly to the English channels including BBC, ITV and Channel Four. If, of course, you can receive their signals.

It's enough to drive a person to drink and rather makes you wonder about the effectiveness of publicly funded organisations, doesn't it?

But that's not all, not by a long shot. If you choose to move to Ireland take note that the Irish government has found an infinite number of other ways of removing the hard-earned money from your wallet.

Take cars, for instance. Not only do we pay twenty one percent VAT on automobile purchases but we also pay another tax (called VRT or Vehicle Registration Tax) that the government created simply to generate additional revenue. Now, Irish citizens pay more than almost anyone else in Europe for the benefits of an automobile. If we could do it we'd all use mass transit. However, getting from A to B can be virtually impossible due to historic under-funding of both railways and the public bus service.

Or how about gasoline? Called petrol over here, Irish car owners are crucified every time they pull into the petrol station for a fill of juice. While a barrel of oil and its derivatives have become more expensive everywhere due to the fracas in the Middle East, the Irish still pay much more than in the U.S., in fact well over twice what the folks in the United States pay for a gallon of gasoline. Why such a difference? You guessed it – taxes.

Combined with extortionate automobile insurance premiums (taxed yet again by the government), in addition to a yearly Car Motor Tax (that can cost anywhere from a couple of hundred euro to over one thousand euro per annum depending on the size of engine you purchase), driving a car in Ireland is exorbitantly expensive.

You could, of course, purchase a bike or take the train or bus if you want to travel from Dublin, say, to Cork. Or you could possibly purchase that donkey and cart but most of us put up with the expense of a car for the simple reason that we need the damned things.

How about cigarettes and alcohol? Do you drink or smoke? Then be prepared to pay for it. We have some of the highest taxes in the EU on these items. Currently we pay over six euro per packet of cigarettes, which means that if you smoke you might consider breaking the habit when coming to Ireland. Mind you, the government has recently banned smoking from almost all public places, so quitting in Ireland is now easier than you might think.

Or what about the price of drink? Ireland, after all, is supposed to be a nation of drinkers and you'd think that the price of a pint would be kept within reasonable reach. Unfortunately, that's just not so. The price of a pint of the best has soared in recent years: a Pint of Plain (the local euphemism for a pint of Guinness) now approaches four euro for the pleasure. That said alcohol prices have actually remained fairly stable recently in that drinkers were already raising hell at the high cost, and while drinking here is much less expensive than in Finland or Switzerland a night out at the pub can still significantly dent your budget.

Or take house purchase taxes. When purchasing a house, Irish nationals (and anyone else for that matter) must pay the government a Stamp Duty. Unless you're a first time buyer (in which case you're exempt from this scurrilous tax) this ruinous fee runs anywhere from three percent of the purchase price of the house – and upward – and must be paid at the time of closing. Budgeting for the purchase of an Irish house? Then you'd best add a few thousand euro to your closing cost line items. Closing costs compared to other countries are crazed. For instance: a friend of mine recently purchased a house in Florida. Closing costs including a few hundred bucks in government taxes came in at approximately two thousand U.S. dollars. Now compare that to Ireland: another friend of mine bought a house only last month. It was a nice-ish house, and she bought it for three hundred thousand euro (about $390,000 at current exchange rates). Her closing costs, including stamp duties and solicitor's fees, came in at over ten thousand euro.

How about Credit Cards? The government has recently enacted a tax on these of forty euro per annum per credit card for the pleasure of saying 'Charge it!' This is yet another example of how the Irish bureaucracy magically materialises more cash for the public coffers.

Of course, we wouldn't mind the high taxes if we were getting value for money from the government. The citizens of many European countries pay high taxes but they receive plenty for it: great medical care, unparalleled unemployment assistance when things go wrong, exceptional public transport...the list goes on and on.

In Ireland, however, and though we pay through the nose, we also wonder what we're receiving in return. Irish taxpayers are a cynical lot, and having for years read about government waste and ineptitude in the newspapers, we really wonder if all of our hard-earned tax moneys are simply being flushed down some far-off government toilet.

The good news is that Irish taxation levels have actually fallen in recent years. The government has started to pay down its substantial debt to international banking institutions, thereby decreasing its significant public borrowings. With any luck, and should fortune continue to smile on the Irish economy, those taxation levels should continue to fall.

But I would be remiss if I did not provide the following warning: Ireland can be expensive. If you land a job – even a good job – life can be something of a struggle. You may not be able to save as much as you're used to saving. Consequently, you must spend more time budgeting and planning personal finances and will need to take a closer look at such important future inevitabilities as the cost of your offspring's college fees and your own imminent retirement, and you must plan accordingly.

But having moved to Ireland, you can always forget about it all by taking a walk in the Irish countryside and breathing that clean Irish air. It's the one thing that the government has yet to figure out how to tax. And please God they never do.

Mind you, I'm sure they're working on it.

Guideline Three
Can't Get a Job? Then Do it Yourself

'This country is a land of entrepreneurs. Because we are now part of the European Union with immediate access to three hundred million consumers, because ownership is part of the Irish nature; because we look for a challenge; because we desire to control our own destinies, new business starts in this country have never been as vibrant. Though working for yourself is challenging and requires a great deal of commitment, there is nothing on this earth quite as satisfying.'

Pat Downey
Company Director

As outlined above, gaining citizenship and the right to work in this country has become a little tricky. Unlike America, Ireland does not have a 'Green Card' lottery system that has allowed so many of its citizens (and the rest of the world) to settle legally in the United States. Rather, the Irish government is protecting its economy by making residency and citizenship more and more difficult to be had by would-be immigrants.

However, there is another road to Irish residency; a method that is not talked about very often and which remains something of a secret. This option presents a personal journey that requires a little more work and risk than most, but that can also be exceptionally fun, financially rewarding, and personally satisfying.

And it's this: *setting up your own business in Ireland.*

If you can create jobs in Ireland – if you can contribute to the Irish economy – the Irish government will almost bend over backwards to make certain that you'll stay here.

The Coming of Irish Entrepreneurship

Ireland has become a country of the self-employed, each hoping to reach their personal financial dreams and sense of self-worth. I should mention that it wasn't always this way. Since the advent of the Irish government and constitution in the 1920's, and due in great part to this country's history of servitude that resulted from a continual stream of invasion and foreign intervention, many Irish people have historically been interested only in job security.

You would be too if your personal dream consisted of only surviving until the next day, hoping to avoid being tossed off your land by a difficult landlord.

For many years, up until the past twenty years or so in fact, Irish parents hoped that their sons and daughters would join the ranks of the Irish civil service or other safe havens such as State owned banks and insurance companies. There, they knew that their progeny would be protected from the harsh difficulties of life. Back in the days of my parents-in-law, obtaining 'a pension-able job' became a catch-phrase symbolising success and achievement.

The problem with such a culture is that it reinforced a risk-free business environment. Most people would not take the personal risk of starting their own business for fear that they would soon be unemployed. While working for a government department, or an Irish bank such as Bank of Ireland or Allied Irish Bank, or within a semi-state company including the P&T (Post and Telegraph, that semi-state body that was years ago responsible for both the post and telephone system), Aer Lingus, or the ESB (Electricity Supply Board, another semi-state that made certain that Ireland produced and delivered enough electricity to serve its own needs) brought a guaranteed paycheque and retirement income, that aspiration to work for a large and risk-less organisation also fostered an unnerving sense of isolation within those organisations. This inevitably resulted in a national business philosophy that led to decay and poor business performance.

Such a business culture can have dire consequences.

When I came here back in 1982 Ireland had firmly established itself as one of the worst performing economies in Europe. Interest rates stood at over fifteen percent. Almost twenty percent of the work force was unemployed. The telephone system didn't work. The rest of Ireland's infrastructure – including the road networks, schools, and health systems – lay rotting in the Irish rain like so many blighted potatoes.

The government knew that it needed to do something. But what?

A Survivor's Guide to Living in Ireland

It took over twenty years to do it but the Irish government – and the people who live here – have managed to turn around business attitudes and the cultural fortresses that rewarded safety. In doing so, they have established a new environment that rewards not only growing businesses, but also the dynamic entrepreneurs that risk all to establish those organisations.

A few of the fundamental actions that resulted in this new climate include the following:

In the 1970's, the IDA (Ireland's Industrial Development Authority) was established with a remit to attract foreign investment. Its personnel took to the roads, visiting the United States, Japan, Germany and other industrial nations with a view to motivating larger global companies to locate part of their operations in Ireland.

Bord Failte, the Irish government's tourism body, was also given some teeth. It began to advertise the joys of visiting Ireland to the peoples of the world. The Irish have always known that their country offers something special. It was now the task of Bord Failte to promote this country, thereby attracting foreign dollars, Deutchmarks, Yen, and other hard currencies into Ireland. Within a few years of the start of their efforts, tourism began to make a real contribution to the local economy.

Next, the government took a hard look at its tax system. Initially, it lowered taxes on corporate profits generated by manufacturing companies to 10 percent. It also made it easier for foreign companies to re-gentrify profits back to company headquarters located abroad.

Ireland also began the process of becoming an active part of European business. As an island nation located somewhere west of London, the movers and shakers of this country had always recognised that few Europeans ever thought of Ireland when considering possible suppliers. Ireland had been one of the original members of the EEC (the European Economic Community) that had been established back in the 1970's. Ireland's government knew that it was imperative to become a participant in any new economic structure that fostered ties with continental Europe and England. They would do anything they could to establish Ireland as a real part of a new emerging Europe.

A Survivor's Guide to Living in Ireland

For many years, Ireland laid the foundations that many hoped would bring a new sense of direction and fiscal well being to this country. Then, over the course of perhaps ten years, and due as much to old-fashioned good luck as to anything else, Ireland's fortunes finally turned.

I remember a couple of the high points. At the time, no one could have really guessed what was heading toward us like a freight train burgeoning with Celtic gold. But looking back, it now all makes perfectly good sense.

In the late 1980's and early 1990's, Ireland suddenly became interesting to much of the world. Ireland's soccer team became a real force in the 1990 World Cup play-offs. While Ireland went crazy (literally) at the superb performance of its team, the soccer-watching citizens of the globe (and there are millions of them) became aware of this country through worldwide television broadcasts. In that Ireland had never been known for the outstanding performance of its sports teams, Europe and much of the rest of the world began to wonder just who these Irish people were.

Also, rock bands such as U2 and outstanding musicians and modern-traditional groups such as Enya and Clannad took the world by storm. As these artists journeyed around the globe, musicians like Bono communicated their vision of a New Ireland. While Ireland had always been known for its poets and writers, those past endeavours were now amplified with a distinctly modern twist. Ireland's enigmatic music touched millions with a contemporary beat and language that soon gave notice to the rest of the world that Ireland was part of the 'now'.

Other artistic endeavours also caused the world press to sit up and wonder. *Riverdance*, that incredibly wonderful dance musical and celebration of Irish culture, caused a ripple of pleasure throughout the world as it began touring to places as far-flung as New York, Sydney and China. With more than eight thousand performances, and seen by over 18 million people, this songfest has helped to convert millions to a new vision of Ireland.

As these small victories began to sweep throughout the globe, they gained column inches in the world press. This ripple effect began to swell, and for the first time in years people from London to Peoria, Beijing to Antwerp, and Berlin to Sydney began to sit up and ask themselves a question: who are these Irish?

Simultaneously, staff within the IDA, Bord Failte, and other Irish investment and public relations organisations turned up the pressure. In boardrooms throughout the world, practical managers of great global business institutions let themselves be won over by the famous Irish charm, the country's accessible location, the intelligence of its citizenry, and of course the substantial tax breaks.

Then, like a story from ancient Irish mythology, and as if the great warrior Cucullain himself had risen from the dead in order to lead the Irish to victory, an amazing storm gathered and for the first time in a millennia everything came together. It was 1995. Ireland's Celtic Tiger was born.

Companies that had been attracted here by the IDA started to invest even further. IBM, Intel, Microsoft, Dell, Hewlett Packard – pick almost any well-known blue chip corporation – started building manufacturing, research & development, and service organisations here. They started hiring. Unemployment fell from 15 percent, to 10 percent, to virtually nil. These multi-national organisations began sourcing more parts, more services, more of everything from local Irish suppliers. And at this writing, those forces are still at work. In the last few months both eBay and Yahoo have decided to locate European business headquarters here.

Local Irish business people – those long-suffering folks who had made do with very little for so many years – bolted out of the starting gates like run-away colts. Existing Irish businesses began to expand. Irish entrepreneurs began to gain confidence. And that confidence spread like wildfire to anyone who thought they might have a plan to make some money on their own.

Until the fires of the Celtic Tiger had been lit, Ireland had always been a country of civil servants, shopkeepers, and farmers. After 1995, it seemed like the entire country wanted to start a business. And so it was that a new culture, a culture of Irish entrepreneurship, was born.

Many countries in Europe put up fences to thwart the entrepreneur. In England, Germany and France (to name a few) managers of small businesses spend hours filling in forms and complying with strict employment rules all the while attempting to keep their businesses afloat. If you are a European with an entrepreneurial bent and are considering a move to Ireland, you will be pleasantly surprised by this country's support of small business. While Irish managers have to put up with assorted red tape and tax compliance issues, we have it relatively easy compared to our European counterparts. And coupled with relatively low business taxes, European business people will view Ireland as a seeming Nirvana.

If you are from the United States you will feel right at home. The U.S. has always been a country that has fostered the entrepreneur. From Benjamin Franklin to Edison to Bill Gates, people from my native country have always dreamed of working for themselves. To Americans, building a business from scratch can seem like second nature. Until the Celtic Tiger, opportunities for establishing a business located in Ireland were limited. But now, Americans, Europeans, and anyone else coming here with a sense of purpose can mine gold from the hills of this new island of opportunity.

By combining your entrepreneurial heritage with a country that now supports the entrepreneur, you too can not only move to Ireland but also stay and prosper. Like so many others.

Ireland as a Centre for Business

Only ten or fifteen years ago a person thinking of setting up his or her own business in Ireland had little choice. They might establish a shop in a local village, buy a pub perhaps, open a Bed & Breakfast for the tourist trade, or otherwise try to ferret out a meagre living to stave off starvation and personal destitution.

It isn't that way anymore. Ireland can now support almost any idea that a person might have, as long as that idea is reasonable and tailored to some notion of reality.

But if you're considering setting up a business here it is best to remember the realities of this country:

Population

The population of the entire island of Ireland, including Northern Ireland, is just about five million souls, or so says the most recent government census. That's less than the population of Los Angeles. Unless you plan to export a product or service abroad (a highly commendable occupation, by the way, and looked upon favourably by a variety of Irish funding agencies), you'd do best to remember that you'll have to pull a living from what is a very small local populace.

In the United States, the United Kingdom, Continental Europe, and many other places, and because of the demographics of these regions, a good idea can make a person wealthy even if that idea is tailored only to the population of the contiguous U.S., the households of England, or the wine growers of France. In Ireland, it is a different matter. While real wealth can be had here, a business strategy that targets only the island of Ireland significantly limits your opportunities.

However, be aware – very aware – that Ireland is a member, and sits within shouting distance, of one of the world's largest and wealthiest economic entities: the European Union. Since its establishment this economic powerhouse has grown rapidly. The current list of Member States consists of: Austria, Belgium, Denmark, Finland, France, Germany, Greece, Ireland, Italy, Luxembourg, Netherlands, Portugal, Spain, Sweden, and the United Kingdom. Recent additions include Cyprus (the Greek part), the Czech Republic, Estonia, Hungary, Latvia, Lithuania, Malta, Poland, Slovakia and Slovenia. And more including Bulgaria, Croatia, Romania, and Turkey have applied to join the EU.

The current Member States already use a common currency – the euro (except Britain, which remains positively dedicated to their British Pound Sterling) – for all transactions. With twenty-five countries comprising a veritable engine of commerce all using the one currency, this economic strategy can only increase common trade among peoples. As time moves on, and Member States come to additional agreements, the European Union will have removed all trade barriers, harmonized most taxation, provided its diverse population with a common citizenship, and will have otherwise created one of the world's greatest economies.

The results of this economic union between nations has already been staggering. Ireland, as just one example, has been the beneficiary of billions of euro worth of grants that has contributed to the development of its economic infrastructure, helping the country to ignite the flames of the Celtic Tiger. Those same benefits are also significantly contributing to the economies of Spain, Greece, Poland, and the rest of the EU. Their citizens are reaping the rewards by becoming wealthier, thereby gaining greater disposable income and economic freedom. As time passes, these hundreds of millions of consumers will demand even more products and services, opening the door for even more small businesses.

The European Union represents tremendous opportunities. And Ireland – sitting at its periphery – is a natural bridge between the vast potential of a combined European economy and the United States. American and European entrepreneurs thinking of relocating to Ireland might consider the opportunities that lie both to the East and West of this small island nation.

Infrastructure

Since my early days here, and the inability to acquire such basics as a telephone without sacrificing my first-born child for the pleasure, Ireland's infrastructure has seen improvements that are mind-blowing. While this country still has a way to go, living here is no longer akin to settling in the deepest wilds of the Amazon. Instead, it's rather like living anywhere in the United States or central Europe except the culture is of course different, the people talk with a different accent, and the back roads are still loaded with potholes (though even that bumpy characteristic is also slowly improving).

But Americans, Europeans, and other nationalities will no longer be shocked by the absence of life's little pleasures. Instead, I suspect that you will be pleasantly surprised by the situation – unless, of course, you were hoping to find a land steeped only in ancient ruins in which case you might be disappointed.

A quick run-down on the improvements to this country:

Telecommunications – on the whole, Ireland now has one of the best pro-business telecom infrastructures in Europe. Broadband, while not yet available everywhere in the country, can be tapped in all major cities including Dublin, Galway, Wexford, Limerick, Cork, Waterford, and other major population centres. The country's telecommunications infrastructure, having rapidly improved, can now support almost any business that requires extensive telecom and web access.

Prices do remain stubbornly high compared to my parents' telephone and broadband bill. But get this: it can now cost less per minute to telephone the United States from Ireland than it is to make a similar call from my old stomping grounds to this country. In a few short years, Ireland has put together one of the best telecommunications systems in Europe. Not only is it about time, but it is also a real pleasure.

Mind you, I do occasionally miss the opportunity of listening in on someone's conversation when the telephone lines managed to get crossed, as they did in the old days.

Roads – new highways and by-ways are being built everywhere. While you must recognise that Ireland is playing catch-up on a history of near-poverty, and though many Irish residents continue to be frustrated by potholed horrors that continue to plague some areas, on the whole the National Roads Authority is making great efforts to improve intra-Ireland transport. For instance, in the past ten years Ireland's Road Authority has spent literally billions of euro on new roadways throughout the country, including miles and miles of dual carriageway. They are also working with local County Councils to repave many of the country roads and within the next few years hope that Ireland's history of jaw-breaking potholes will be a thing of the past.

International Access – the Irish government, as well as local and international transport companies, continue to improve access to and from this country. International airports – with access to Europe, the United States, and other global destinations – include Dublin, Shannon (in County Clare) and Cork. Other local airports (Galway, Knock, Kerry and Donegal) serve local needs and provide feeder airline service to main airport hubs, with some feeding directly to a variety of U.K. and Continental destinations.

Ferry services from Cork, Rosslare and Dublin provide direct sea transport to the U.K. and Continental Europe. The road network supports truck transport from any part of the country to these ports in order to facilitate export requirements.

In short, Ireland is no longer a European backwater. Due to its improved transportation network and telecommunications infrastructure, companies from as far a-field as the United States, Japan, Australia, Germany, France, the rest of Europe – and the world – are finding it increasingly easier, and less expensive, to locate to this country.

Taxation – the past few governments have substantially lowered taxation on business. Most businesses now attract only 12.5 percent tax on corporate profits (the ten percent corporation profit tax was raised a few years ago but the government plans on holding the new rate for the foreseeable future). While personal taxation remains stubbornly high compared to the United States, many businesses are locating here due to these incredibly low levels of corporation profits tax. If you establish a business here, you'll attract a similarly low level of tax. The goal, then, is to figure out how to keep those profits in your pocket.

Grants & Assistance – Ireland has established a number of government agencies whose remit is to support the growth and viability of indigenous Irish businesses. These agencies include the IDA and Enterprise Ireland. A contact list is provided in the Reference section at the back of this book.

The point of all this is that, after many years of centralised mayhem, Ireland has at last become a country whose remit former U.S. President Calvin Coolidge would have admired: the business of Ireland really does seem to be business.

Now we'll start to look at how you can use this new economic reality to help make your dream of living in Ireland come true.

Opportunities for the Entrepreneur

You should know that in 1987 I took the plunge and decided to become a real honest-to-God Irish entrepreneur. I am decidedly *not* a born businessperson. I suspect that the entrepreneurial gene was decidedly absent from my makeup. In fact, the thought of setting up on my own scared me silly.

Back in 1987, I had little choice. At that time the country was in a downward economic spiral and the chances of a quick recovery were highly unlikely. Back then, and having finally left my lowly paid position as a weighbridge salesman, I landed a job with a division of the Hyster Forklift Company, a subsidiary of the U.S. multi-national. The subsidiary was based just north of Dublin and I'd had the good fortune to find work there as a marketing type, albeit for a salary that was still barely adequate to keep our household afloat.

Once ensconced in my job, however, and having had the time to look around, I decided that things didn't look too good for the company. Not by half. The Hyster operation was funding itself almost wholly from Irish grants. Its mission to develop a series of automated guided vehicles was coming off the rails and its booked sales were not meeting targets nor contributing to overheads. I quickly became aware of the fact that the company had only a short time to survive

I knew that if I didn't do something about it there was a good possibility that I was going to end up back on the dole queue. Of course I thought about getting another job. But upon looking around it transpired that few were hiring. Those that were had no cause to hire an American. They had their own families and friends to think about.

Consequently, and facing impending unemployment head-on, I decided to take a careful – though frightening – look at establishing my own business.

When I first considered setting up a business in this country, and because I was not a shopkeeper, farmer, or civil servant, I thought that the only industries that might be open to me were one of those wee little cottage companies that dot the west coast of this country like so many clumps of multi-coloured heather. You know the ones: pottery making, knitting, painting, tourist brick-a-brack. Being an American, I automatically thought that the only real opportunities were going to be found serving the tourist market.

Needless to say, I was not a potter, knitter, or painter and immediately bemoaned my fate. I thought that I would never, ever be able to develop my own business. I was wrong.

In my case, I established a marketing and communications company. Looking back on it, the entire experience was – at first anyway – absolutely terrifying. I took on a partner (a fellow American as it turned out) and we beat a path to every large blue chip organisation in the country, attempting to sell a not-yet-quite-developed expertise in direct mail and similar direct response advertising techniques.

For a while, and despite my foreboding, things went well. Initially, we established ourselves as a joint venture with a major Dublin-based advertising agency. Having purchased a certain credibility, we grew quickly. In 1989 we bought out the joint venture partner's shareholding and traded independently. We moved into larger premises. We took on more staff. We increased our capabilities.

In 1990, however, George Bush Senior decided to bomb Iraq. Within days, our source of revenue from blue chip clients – revenue that had taken years to develop – had dried up. I watched as those years of toil imploded. The company went into liquidation in early 1991.

In 1992, I tried again. This time I took a less ambitious approach. I set up completely on my own. I sold a variety of marketing capabilities again, but this time I sold them to a wider range of companies – smaller organisations, the occasional blue chip, anything to get by.

This time things have gone well. Almost fourteen years later we are still in business. I employ only a handful of other people and have kept my company and its overhead structure quite small, and yet we have always managed to make a profit. The combination of low overheads and careful planning seems to have worked in this country, and to the benefit of my family and fellow employees.

But my main point is this: I never thought of myself as an entrepreneur. Though I went to business school as a graduate student I always thought that my career path would consist of remaining an employee, attached to someone else's burning star.

Once again, I was wrong. And if I can make it here in my own business, I like to think that any global citizen with a strong sense of commitment and personal motivation can make it too.

As you consider your options keep in mind that many business segments within Ireland are continuing to grow at four percent per annum and more. This gives plenty of scope for development. Doubly keep in mind that certain industries are growing faster than others. These include:

Home Construction

Every person in this country seems to be climbing onto the property ladder. Due to today's demographics – the fact that the majority of Irish citizens are younger, setting up families, and otherwise beginning that wonderful struggle called Living – the country has been swept up in a tidal wave of home buying.

41

Contractors and other firms established to serve this incredible demand for new housing are getting rich. If you're a carpenter, plumber, electrician, contractor, framer, sales agent, or otherwise have skills in this area, and if you can quickly learn what it takes to meet the specific requirements of the home construction market in Ireland, you could get rich by setting up a home construction company here.

Of interest to would-be North American entrepreneurs in this segment is the fact that Irish tastes in homes are changing. For years and years, Irish houses were constructed of poured concrete and breezeblocks. Only recently has this market started looking at wooden framed houses – construction techniques that were adopted by U.S. builders years ago.

Wood construction techniques, and that includes standard framed houses, A-Frame homes, and Log Cabin type construction, are now all the rage. If you have experience in this area you could be onto a winner.

Additional Construction Related Industries

While we're examining homes, let's talk about those segments that support that primary industry, as well as Home Improvement.

If you have skills in anything from landscape architecture and design to outdoor deck construction; interior design to carpet and tile supply and fitting, you may well prosper here. Because of recent changes in Irish consumer tastes, more and more people are transforming their homes into palaces that many Americans or Europeans would immediately appreciate.

Under floor heating, outdoor decking, in-built spas, redesigned and landscaped yards (called 'gardens' this side of the Pond), conservatories, complete extensions, redesigned and redecorated interiors, comprehensive home refurbishments, and all of the supporting elements that these products and services require are in constant demand.

Irish people want nicer homes. Just as importantly, they have the vision – and money – to obtain the mansions of their dreams. So if you have the skills and experience that can help meet these demands, you can consider this entire industry as ripe with opportunity. I'll give you two quick examples of people who are succeeding in this area, both in the tile trade:

A neighbour of mine recently emigrated from Italy. Having worked in the Italian home tile industry for years, he set out to establish an Irish company for himself.

He started importing tiles directly from his home country. His products are absolutely beautiful (I know – my wife insisted that we retile the kitchen using his products) and he has quickly built a company and a good living completely on word of mouth.

The second tale is a quick one involving a Tiler, also from Italy. A friend of the tile importer above, this man – who can only speak a few words of English – and his wife are now subcontracted to lay all of the aforementioned Italian tile. His name is Roberto; her name is Maria. They are a delightful couple who work very hard and who laid the tile in our kitchen. They worked their butts off and laid that exceptional tile in a way that was absolutely beautiful.

My wife and I were so pleased that we started recommending the couple to the neighbours. Now these two hard working immigrants can expect a harvest of continuing work just from our neighbourhood. They work so hard that I suspect they will be greeted with a consistent demand for their talents from homeowners throughout the area.

The above examples illustrate two points: first, if you have a skill that can be tied into the housing industry, you're onto a winner. Second, if you know someone in Ireland that is already supplying this area, and if you have a skill that can support that existing business, you'll be in a much better position to quickly mine this opportunity.

Computer Support

Ireland has become a country driven by the computer. Like much of the rest of the developed world, every company and individual now seems to have at least one PC, and sometimes two, three, four or more.

And where you find computers, you'll also find computer problems that create opportunities for those in the know.

Within the broader computer support industry, IT security possibly presents the greatest opportunity. I have a close friend who works in this area, and he is building a wonderfully profitable IT security business on the back of those idiots who are generating Spam, porn, computer viruses and the like.

If you have the knowledge that can help reduce – or eliminate – the above-mentioned curses to Irish and international computer users, you should be able to quickly develop a profitable enterprise.

Additionally, Irish companies (and individuals) are also investing heavily in new computer hardware and software including everything from comprehensive LAN systems to simple firewalls. While you will undoubtedly want to avoid those areas that are already over-supplied, and which attract low margins (computer hardware, for instance), you will certainly do well by developing services that support newer technologies. Computer consultants who understand LAN, WiFi, firewall technology and software, and similar technologies are currently cleaning up.

Of perhaps even more interest is the fact that many small entrepreneurs are developing software products ripe for international export. *The Sunday Business Post* (Ireland's favourite newspaper for the smaller to mid-sized entrepreneur; you can find them at www.sbpost.ie) is consistently filled with articles about those individuals who had an idea to mine the opportunities inherent in the computer industry, and have subsequently made a fortune.

Irish entrepreneurs are now selling their computer-based expertise to countries throughout the world.

Health Care

Nurses & Doctors: first, if you're a qualified nurse or doctor and want to come to Ireland, know that you should have little difficulty in getting a job. You will, of course, need to examine certification requirements (your existing license may not be valid in this country), but Ireland is in frantic need for people with these skills – particularly nurses.

Recently, for instance, Ireland started recruiting abroad for nurses to meet immediate vacancies. If you're interested in this area, my only advice is to examine any contract that you are offered. Recently, Irish newspapers carried stories concerning Filipino nurses that were only granted a one-year's contract – and work permit to match. Needless to say, these highly skilled individuals were not pleased by the lack of job security.

Alternative Medicines: the Irish have embraced alternative medicines with great enthusiasm. So much so that there now exist huge opportunities for entrepreneurs. Consider Ki Massage, Reiki Healing techniques, Native American sweathouses – anything that offers a spiritual alternative to traditional medicinal techniques.

Additionally, a number of Irish companies have established a whole range of manufacturing capabilities, supplying a spectrum of vitamins, essential oils, whole grain foodstuffs, low fat and no fat food substitutes, and similar healthy consumer goods, to meet the demands generated by Irish and international consumers.

Many of these companies are now exporting their products to Europe. Europeans love Irish food and alternative medicine exports simply because Ireland has always positioned itself as a land of clean air and clean living. Irish exports within this area are usually greeted with open wallets.

The Food Industry

If alternative medicines are not your bag, consider the wide variety of opportunities available in the food industry.

As mentioned above, many perceive Ireland as a country that fosters purity and all that goes with it. Consumers throughout the world continue to believe that Ireland's pure waters, rich soil, and relatively clean air help this country to create some of the best food products anywhere.

Though some of those beliefs are now suspect (the danger of pollution often goes hand-in-hand with economic growth), that thinking is for the most part still correct.

Entrepreneurs who have had the vision to develop new and useful food products have gone on to make fortunes. New businesses serving niche product categories including spring water, chocolate, cheese, yoghurt and other dairy products, mustard, whiskey and spirits, natural beer, wine (yes, some entrepreneurs have managed to grow grapes in this northern country), biscuits and crackers, and many other foodstuffs have prospered.

The fishing industry also continues to be ripe with opportunity. While European fishing quotas have resulted in fewer fish being swept from the sea (giving them a chance to reproduce and thereby guaranteeing a fishing industry for Ireland's progeny) value-added products focusing on fish and shellfish continue to play an important part in Ireland's economy. An entrepreneur who has a good idea that results in new pre-packed fish dishes delivered to Irish and European grocery stores could very well find him or herself rewarded with precious pearls.

Do you have a penchant for creating new recipes? Can you think of something unique to offer the rest of the world? If so, you may not only find that you can make a fortune, but also make your dream of living in Ireland come true as well.

Franchise Opportunities

Franchises have been great wealth creators within Ireland. Of interest is the fact that many well-known franchise opportunities are already available on these shores. But a number of famous franchises have not yet made it to Ireland and may be interested in coming here – which could offer you an incredible opportunity.

Fast Food: McDonald's and Burger King, two American stalwarts, have already surged into the Irish market as the result of changing Irish tastes. McDonald's in particular is seeing quick growth in this country and are on the lookout for new franchise operators. While you may not want to take part in a Mac's franchise, feeling that it represents U.S. global opportunism, it is a fact that this company is helping Irish franchise operators to grow wealthy.

Other Irish-originated franchise opportunities within the Fast Food segment are also available including O'Brien's Sandwiches and SuperMac's (a home-grown competitor to McDonald's). Both are seeking to expand through franchise agreements.

Coffee Bars

Many people often think that the Irish drink nothing but tea and Guinness. While the Irish penchant for a pint is still true, the Irish have managed to change their tastes regarding non-alcoholic beverages. Though the Guinness Book of Records maintains that Ireland is still the top tea drinker in the world, the Irish are also a nation of firm coffee drinkers. Recent research indicates that the Irish drink about as much coffee as they do tea – a change in consumer behaviour that would have seemed unthinkable only a few years ago.

Because of this shift in demand, most cities and larger towns now have their share of coffee bars – and a few individuals are getting rich by establishing chains that supply espresso, cappuccino and the like.

If you believe that you have the talent to serve a meaner cappuccino, then perhaps this is the route for you.

Call Centre Support

You've undoubtedly read the news that many U.S. and European companies are exporting service support jobs to lower cost economies, particularly India. This, of course, is quite true. What you may not know is that for many years a number of international companies have established similar call centre and back-office support operations in Ireland.

Things have changed, of course, and this trend isn't as popular as it was only a few years ago. This is due to the simple fact that Ireland is no longer a low cost economy. Skilled people here demand wages that are equal to – and often more expensive – than their U.S. or European counterparts.

However, due to a number of factors including the significant improvement in Irish telecommunications infrastructure, the fact that all Irish people speak excellent English, the fact that many Irish have fluency in French, German, and other European languages, the additional fact that those same people have often experienced an exceptional standard of general education, the mere five-hour time difference between Dublin and New York City, and the proximity to the European continent, this area still offers opportunity.

Obviously, and due to the wage situation here, call centres that are price sensitive will not be economically viable in Ireland. However, centres that support higher priced goods and services (such as those supporting the computer or insurance industries) and that can support a higher overhead structure continue to attract interest.

Software Development

Ireland has become a Mecca for anyone with a penchant in this area. Having become a Silicon Valley for western Europe, Ireland now possesses people, skill sets and infrastructure that promotes software development across a wide spectrum: everything from games for handheld devices including cell phones and PDA's to the latest in security software.

The Irish government is continuing to throw money at this strategic growth area. New developments in the Liberties area of Dublin, including a fully-fledged R&D facility supported by centralised high-bandwidth broadband telecommunications capabilities, are now attracting both start-up and operating companies. A variety of grants are also available to support this growing commercial sector.

International Export Opportunities

Ireland continues to export more than it imports. For instance, recent statistics suggest that Ireland is the largest exporter of software in the world.

Exports continue to be critical to the growth of the Irish economy and they are now the engines for continuing economic success. While industries that serve only the Irish market can be eligible for government support, those processes and products that have export potential are more likely to receive grant support from Irish government agencies such as Ireland's Enterprise Board.

Today, Ireland's economy exports a wide variety of products – and skills – to many other nations throughout Europe, North America, China, Africa, and beyond. Exports include (but are not limited to): software, live and slaughtered cattle, value-added food products, mushrooms, potatoes, furniture, fish and value-added fish product, consultancy services serving the duty-free area (Irish business people developed the duty-free concept and continue to service that area), electric power plant design and development, construction consulting, aero-space engineering expertise, pharmaceuticals, pottery, crystal, and alcoholic beverages including liquor and beer.

If you have a business model that incorporates an export capability, the Irish government may support that concept with valuable grants and loans.

Financial Services

In the late 1970's, then-Taoiseach Charles Haughey (Ireland's Prime Minister) began to develop a compelling financial services model that he believed would turn Ireland into an international financial powerhouse. Though it took a few years to reach fruition, his dream has been turned into reality with the development of the Irish Financial Services Centre (IFSC).

Located in Dublin on the north side of the River Liffey, this centre offers a variety of tax breaks to international financial services companies (and other qualifying companies) including: Corporation tax at 10 percent on trading profits, a 10-year exemption from municipal taxes, double rent allowances for leased property, 100 percent depreciation allowances for commercial buildings, plant and machinery, and no withholding taxes on dividends or interest. Since its inception, the IFSC has been attracting large-scale blue chip companies and more modest financial services operations including banking, insurance, re-insurance, stock trading, and money management companies, like a magnet.

This influx of well-known organisations has resulted in a number of opportunities for the individual and entrepreneur.

IFSC-based companies are sweeping up people with financial services backgrounds and can't seem to get enough of them. If you have experience in financial services, you may qualify to receive a work permit.

Entrepreneurs are also profiting by setting up support operations that feed into these large-scale financial services companies. Everything from software support to customer relationship marketing expertise is required by these operations.

On Being an Artist

While in office, Charles Haughey also decided to support those participating in the arts with an incredible tax incentive known as the Artist Exemption. With a stroke of his pen, he changed the law to state that income derived by artists from certain sources including creative writing and painting would not be subject to personal taxation.

Since then, Ireland has proven to be a tax haven for writers, painters, and other qualifying artists and their income. Since this law was passed, any number of people plying their skills in the arts has made Ireland their home.

If you derive your income from the arts, you may qualify. Getting an Artist Exemption can be somewhat difficult, but once you have one – and unless the powers that be overturn the law – you will have it for life.

Contact the Irish Revenue Commission (www.revenue.ie) for more information.

Other Opportunities

If you have a skill or a dream and you think it might work in Ireland, than by all means consider it. Though I've skipped tourism in the above list of possible opportunities, this business segment continues to offer exciting prospects for those who are willing to work hard and take a risk.

Possible opportunities include: the establishment of commercial websites that both promote Ireland and tourism niche areas; the purchase of local Bed & Breakfast operations or pubs; the establishment of local tourism companies whose mission it is to attract visitors from particular geographic areas in North America, Europe, or other countries to visit Ireland; and the development of small-scale cottage industries to produce local product for the tourist market.

I've met many immigrants who have settled in this country and who really are spinning both pottery – and their personal dreams and fortunes – at wooden wheels while getting the most out of their lives.

The point of it all is this: if you really want to try working for yourself Ireland offers the opportunity to do just that. You may not get rich in the process, but you'll enjoy the journey.

Some Advice on Doing Business in Ireland

Before moving on, a quick piece of advice – and it's this: the Irish, like any other nationality, love good service. Whatever you do, make certain that you under-promise and over-deliver.

When I first came here service in almost any business operation was pretty abysmal. From manufacturing to retail, companies just didn't seem to give a damn about making sure that their customers were happy. The reasons for this were simple: first, the dismal island economy fostered a business environment of non-existent competition. If you became fed up with the local grocery store, for instance, you had little option of going elsewhere simply because there wasn't anywhere else to go. But as importantly, and at that point, the Irish didn't know how to complain very effectively which meant that Irish businesses had no real reason to get off their butts to make life easier for their Irish consumers.

Things have changed. Because of the recent vibrancy of the economy, hundreds and hundreds of new businesses have set up shop and the winds of healthy competition now blow strongly through Ireland. With the coming of new choices, the Irish realise that they now have some real options and can vote with their feet if they don't like what they are receiving. And though they still have a little bit to learn, Irish consumers are becoming both street-wise and knowledgeable. If they don't get good service, if they think they've been ripped-off or otherwise offended, they'll let you know pretty damned quick.

Most companies within the country have responded well to this demand. Let's face it – this new attitude of the Irish meant that unless businesses got their acts together, their consumers would go elsewhere.

That said, and in my experience, companies still under-perform in ensuring that their existing customers remain happy. In short, and though things have improved, few Irish companies truly embrace a philosophy that includes exceptional customer service.

And this leaves a niche wide open. If you are determined to set up in this country, start from the very beginning by over-servicing your customers. Tell people the truth, make good service a part of your strategy, be on time when delivering a product or going to a meeting (the Irish are prone to being late and appreciate timeliness), come in at a fair price, make your terms known, and be certain that your customers understand those terms and stick to them. Having made everyone happy, make sure that you get referrals. Word of mouth goes a long way in this country.

If you make certain that everyone is happy you'll quickly achieve that level of success that you're hoping for. And the Irish will love you for it.

Your Right to Remain in this Country

As stated above, and unless you are already an EU citizen or can prove ancestral Irish blood, North Americans and citizens from other parts of the world can now find it difficult to obtain a Visa to live here.

However, if you create jobs in this country it's an entirely different matter. In that the Irish government is promoting job creation they will look most favourably upon your decision to develop a business that serves the employment and tax creation needs of the country.

Recently, I talked to an individual within an international office of the IDA regarding 'illegal' immigrants who set up a business within Ireland but who had not yet received an appropriate Visa from the Irish government. The IDA official, while circumspect, made it known that government officials would view favourably those individuals who were creating jobs and generating tax revenue for government coffers.

Those individuals who choose to invest in this country will, for a while anyway, be living in something of a phantom zone in that they will not have any true legal status. For months, they may have to flit back and forth from Ireland to their home nation, while managing their new businesses on the fly. But should these new entrepreneurs continue to create jobs and pay taxes they will eventually be welcomed by the Irish government as legal residents. After a few more years, these individuals will also have the opportunity to apply for citizenship, should they so desire.

The point is clear: if you are willing to set up a business in Ireland, your dream of permanently moving here is within your grasp.

Guideline Four
How I Bought Myself a Little Corner of the Irish Dream

San Francisco, California   *December 12, 1982*

My dear son,

I am writing this in the closet, the paper lit only by a candle, because your father has vowed never to talk to you again and this is the only way that I can pen a message to you so as not to upset him.

As your mother, I must say that I am truly in despair. Did I do something terrible to you when you were a child to have caused such misery that you must now seek revenge? When Ronald (a lovely man) wrote to your father and told him that you had actually purchased a house over there, and were less likely than ever to return home, I thought that Daddy was going to have a heart attack. How you could ever leave our spacious suburban house for the cold of Ireland is simply beyond me.

I enclose twenty dollars. Buy yourself a knit hat, will you please?

Your loving Mother

Having found a job by hook or by crook, your next step toward fulfilling your Irish dream will probably revolve around the purchase of your own Irish sanctuary. At least that's what I did.

Buying a house in any country can be an exciting, though often fraught, journey of discovery and self-preservation. As perhaps the largest purchase a person will ever make, buying a home is a reflection of self and family, an expression of upbringing and personal ambition. Moreover, the type of house purchased seems to be determined by a number of factors: lifestyle and self-image; family size and age; hobbies and interests; financial wherewithal and investment awareness; and perhaps as importantly, the dreams and aspirations that we all live for.

More than any other purchase, home-ownership is an emotionally charged experience. We can all become frighteningly carried away by our own imaginations. Our sense of reality can be confused by dulcet imaginings that only a movie director might construct. We might see ourselves living in a mansion complete with waiter, cook, gardener, and assorted staff to take care of our every need. The reality, however, can often be in stark contrast to the cobweb of wishes that we develop on any dark and lonely evening, while pondering our ambitions over a short glass of whiskey. While we desire the luxury of genteel living, we may discover that our bank balance can only fund a hovel.

When I came to Ireland and considered purchasing a home here I too let my imagination run wild. Ruminating over a bottle of cheap plonk in the dingy house that we had rented – the only place that we could afford – I imagined that my family would be quickly ensconced in rural surroundings like that of an Irish fable. As with John Wayne in *The Quiet Man*, I too would own a thatch cottage surrounded by acres of wooded property, a quiet brook singing to us as it trickled tranquilly over moss-covered stone, and a local pub located within an easy walk through verdant green fields.

Needless to say, I found that my dreams were quickly shattered. Irish housing prices and much of the administrative routine of making a purchase has changed since 1982, but perhaps the following might indicate the processes that my young family – and this ignorant American – went through as we sought our Irish dream home.

I should explain that since arriving here I have lived in what used to be the small sleepy town of Navan. Located in the middle of County Meath and situated approximately thirty miles north of Dublin, it is no longer a sleepy town because the recent economic boom has turned it into a traffic-clogged nightmare. But back then it was quiet enough.

My wife's parents also live here, or did until they both unfortunately passed-away. Because Bernadette was born here, had friends here, and felt a part of the place she didn't want to live anywhere else. Upon our arrival she had made the irrevocable decision that there was only one place to live in Ireland and that was in Navan.

'Couldn't we live in Dublin?' I had croaked upon realising that I was to live in what then was a backwater of a town for what would probably be the rest of my life. 'Dublin has universities. It has wonderful theatres. It has life, for God's sake.'

A Survivor's Guide to Living in Ireland

'Dublin smells,' she had replied. 'Besides, Navan is a wonderful place to live.'

Possibly. I was about to find out. And I did. I was to also discover that my initial assumption about the town was the correct one: back in 1982 Navan really was an Irish backwater. My second assumption was also correct: I've lived here ever since.

When I first immigrated to Ireland, Navan had one major employer: Tara Mines. This zinc mine, the largest mine of its type in Europe, apparently had enough zinc reserves to keep the world going for a million years or so. Back in 1982 the entire town depended on it.

Navan at that point looked like something out of a World War II black and white documentary. It held ten thousand people living in small damp houses that resembled the working set of a Depression Era movie. It had a few schools, three churches (two Catholic and one Church of Ireland Church just to keep the few Protestants happy), a main street full of run-down shops, a couple of fish and chip joints managed by Italian immigrants who constantly complained about the weather and who continually chattered about the brilliant prospects of the Italian football team, one Chinese restaurant that produced fairly reasonable food, two cinemas both of which smelled of mould and were in need of immediate demolition, a brand new shopping centre that to my eye looked already to require refurbishment, and well over thirty pubs.

On weekends the pubs were mobbed as the local miners tried to forget what they did for a living. The locals would all pile in on a dreary, wind-swept Friday evening then engage in a pub crawl throughout the rest of the weekend. A pub crawl, while it might sound obscure, is self-explanatory: drink in one establishment until you get bored then move on to the next public house just to see if the conversation there was more interesting. Navan had over thirty pubs so a conversationalist had plenty of choice. By the time your money ran out you would find yourself crawling on hands and knees to your final destination, undoubtedly passing out and puking in the street before getting there.

If you were lucky a friend or passing Navanite would find you and call the local constabulary who would kindly escort you safely home. Hence the origins of the phrase. I have survived a pub-crawl

55

or two in my lifetime and I can vouch for it as a time-honoured profession.

During the working week, of course, the pubs were as quiet as churches because everyone had already spent their pay packet and couldn't afford a pint of Guinness despite the fact that it sold for a mere sixty pence in old money – about a buck a pint. Come Monday morning, everyone would descend into the zinc mines or otherwise go to their places of employment in order to work their posteriors off so that they could start the process all over again.

Navan was an eye-opener to me. The streets were full of potholes that could take the fillings out of your mouth. The paths ('sidewalks' to North Americans) were broken and filled with weeds, and street lighting was almost non-existent. The telephone system wasn't even a system. It was, I suspected, a work in progress that would not be finished for another twenty years.

When I first came here, and though as previously mentioned it has improved immeasurably since then, I discovered that acquiring a telephone was akin to obtaining the status of royalty. Not only would I have to pay five hundred pounds (close to seven hundred bucks at the time) for installation but I also discovered that having paid this ruinous fee it would take almost six months to have said telephone installed. Once installed, the damned thing rarely worked. If it did you were almost certain to be cut off in mid-sentence or had the dubious pleasure of overhearing Mrs Kelly, a woman on the far side of town, talking about her sister in a most unfortunate turn of phrase. On those rare occasions when you did get through you commenced to pay some of the most outrageously expensive call charges on the face of the globe.

Needless to say, the newly immigrated Richards' clan did without a telephone for well over a year. This was a terrible surprise to a middle-classed American used to running down to the Phone Company, paying his twenty-five bucks, and then hauling a brand new touch-tone into his apartment whereupon he would plug it into an obscure fixture in the wall to be instantly connected to the rest of the world.

In 1982 Ireland, that wasn't going to happen.

Back then Navan was fairly typical of the rest of Ireland. The town is much like the Peoria of the country in that if it's true in Navan it's probably true in the rest of the Irish Republic. Navan was poor. I wouldn't say destitute – no, not that bad. But it was difficult enough. Almost twenty percent of the town – and the country within which it nestled – was unemployed. A productive day out was standing for a couple of hours in the rain outside the unemployment office, waiting for the weekly dole. The entire country was suffering from one of the worst recessions in living memory and no one seemed to know what to do about it. Except the government, of course, and all that they did was raise taxes and declare that we'd just have to put up with it all.

Few people owned cars. Fewer had a garage in which to put them. Most people made their way around the town on foot, which felt wrong somehow but which, over the years, I began to appreciate. Back in America, and if I wanted to buy some donuts, I'd hop into my Chevy, turn the key, and drive the four blocks to Johnny's Donuts where the smiling Vietnamese lady would plop twelve waistline-expanding items into a large box. In Ireland, I didn't have a car because I couldn't afford it. I couldn't go to Johnny's or anything like it because donuts weren't, except in rare instances, available. The Irish did have absolutely yummy cream cakes that we used to purchase on special occasions such as when my parents came over on a misbegotten visit but that was about it. If we wanted them, we'd walk the half-mile into town and get them. My feet hardened into steel bricks but I can say that I felt much better for it all the same.

When we first ventured to this side of the Pond I had determined that we would rent a fine house in a fine estate then take our time to look for that dream home that I longed for. Unfortunately, few rentals were available back then and those houses that were for rent seemed to be owned by landlords that cared little for the health of their tenants.

Our fully-furnished semi-detached rental house was damp, mouldy, came with central heating that we couldn't afford to run, was accessorised with wood-framed windows that had been attacked by wood rot so much so that they were in danger of falling out, and whose floors were covered by mouldering orange and green carpeting that looked as if it had been around since the days of Saint Patrick.

Because of the dismal state of our rental house, and firmly believing that the health and lives of our entire family depended on quickly relocating anywhere else, my wife and I determined to purchase a home as quickly as we could.

With little fanfare, the process was started.

We looked and looked. Being of low financial means, we found that our choice was limited because of the scant money that we had in our pocket. Having eventually found a job, those choices were limited even further by the fact that, due to my obscenely low wages, I simply could not afford a large mortgage.

Looking back on it I now realize that what we should have done was to have borrowed up to the hilt and to hell with the consequences. For instance, we viewed a lovely two-storey farmer's cottage complete with outbuildings built on a couple of acres of land and located at the top of a gloriously windswept hill. It held sweeping views of the Boyne Valley and at the time could be had for a mere thirty-two thousand Irish pounds (about forty thousand U.S. dollars). Today, that same property recently sold for over ten times as much.

However, back then and like most, we simply didn't have the money. So we had to make do. Irish property – then and now – offered a short spectrum of house types:

Bungalows – are defined as stand-alone homes, usually one-storey, usually built on a larger plot of land (often on a quarter acre or more), and most often located in the country.

Estate, or Detached, Homes – usually defined as a typical 'neighborhood' in the United States, are either one or two-storey stand-alone homes, usually available in only one model type, and all residing in a single area, usually built by a single contractor.

Semi-Detached Homes – often known as a townhouse in the U.S., Semi-D's as they are affectionately called over here are two houses built together and having one common wall. Often an entire estate (neighbourhood) will be composed of nothing but Semi-D's, all of the same model type. Semi-detached homes, the most popular type of house in Ireland due to their affordability, are often comprised of three or four bedrooms, a living room-cum-dining room, kitchen, one or two bathrooms, and often a one car garage. Square footage is usually limited to approximately 1500 square feet or less.

Terraced Homes – kind of, sort of, 'condominiums' (depending on your location in the U.S.), this house type has gone out of fashion in Ireland and few are currently being constructed.

Terraced homes are built in a continuous line of anywhere between four and ten dwellings. Each has two common walls (except for the two end houses, of course, which only have one common wall), which means that you share the wall structure with your adjoining neighbours. Terraced houses come in one and two storey versions and are usually quite small, perhaps only a thousand square feet or less, comprised of two or three bedrooms, a kitchen, a bathroom, and a living area. Many terraced houses were built in the early 20th Century as public, or Council, homes. These houses were owned by the various County Councils (county government agencies) and were provided to local tenants at exceptionally low rental rates.

Over the years, most council houses have been purchased by their tenants and can now be sold on a 'freehold' basis by the owner to any purchaser who might be interested.

Manor Houses, Castles, and Unique Homes – Ireland also has its fair share of gracious homes set in locations that are right out of a textbook on faeries and folklore. Castles dating from the 13th Century, complete with thick stone walls and populated by assorted ghosts, sometimes become available on the Irish property market.

Manor Houses (also known as Great Houses) were built at the time of early English rule by Anglo feudal lords who were rewarded for their energetic subjugation of the Irish with substantial land grants. These beautiful homes, often using Georgian architecture, not only feature elegant window fascia and wonderfully plastered ceilings but also often come complete with sweeping staircases and unique internal features. Typically, they rest on large plots of land, much of which has been developed into elegant gardens.

Additionally, Ireland has its fair share of unique homes that have been designed by professional architects to the original owner's requirements and specifications. These occasionally come on the market and can attract great interest by not only the local population but also those erstwhile potential immigrants from the United States, Germany, Italy, England, and the rest of the world.

But getting back to the search for our Irish Dream Home:

Having made the decision to purchase a house, we visited the local realtor, known as an 'Auctioneer' or 'Estate Agent' in this part of the world. Having determined our limited means, he proceeded to inform us that our meagre budget would only allow us to consider the purchase of a Terraced Home. As it happened, he had only one on his books.

In that we were desperate we immediately began the process of purchasing.

It's been so long since I've lived in the U.S. that I forget the machinations of home purchase there. I do, however, remember it to be a frustrating process. It's no less frustrating in Ireland and seems to take months to complete.

The owner of the Terraced House was asking seventeen thousand Irish pounds for his turn of the century, somewhat dilapidated, two bedroom, one toilet house. We bid sixteen-five. He wouldn't take it. We bid sixteen, seven-fifty. He remained firm. We finally offered him the asking price and he accepted.

We provided our Auctioneer with a cheque for the required ten percent deposit and then the fun began.

First, we had to hire a lawyer (known as a solicitor in this part of the world). Our solicitor contacted the owner's solicitor. Various papers went back and forth and forth and back. Initially, the title for the property could not be found. It turned out to be lying in the dusty cabinets of the County Council and it transpired that the house had never been properly registered as a private home, but still resided on the council books as a public Council house. It took weeks – and money – to have the home re-registered.

We also applied to a local bank for a mortgage. At the time, interest rates were a mere seventeen percent per annum and the suspicious bank manager looked askance at providing a sixteen thousand pound mortgage to a young maverick such as me who in all probability would never be in a financial position to maintain his mortgage repayments. However, with pleading smiles and a few warm words from my wife (the fact that she had been raised in the town undoubtedly influenced his decision), the bank manager finally agreed to lend us the money.

Now in possession of mortgage approval, we knew that the rest of the purchase process could proceed. In my ignorance, I firmly believed that such a process would be quick. I was to be proven wrong in my thinking. For a further three months the solicitor that we engaged to look after the closing of this transaction swapped a variety of mysterious paperwork with the seller's solicitor, activity that seemed to have little to do with the purchase of the house but which could have been more concerned with pumping up the price of the solicitor's fees. My young family, still living in the damp rat hole of a rental home, became desperate.

Finally, when it appeared that we would all die of hypothermia, our solicitor contacted us. 'Congratulations. You can pick up the key,' he stated. My wife shrieked in exaltation.

In Ireland picking up a key to a new home is cause for wild celebration. Greeting card companies sell 'Congratulations on Your New Home!' cards for just such occasions. My wife was crazed with excitement and we withdrew to the local pub for a well-deserved drink.

Having received the key, we immediately took occupancy. And that's when the trouble really started. The previous owner, contrary to contract, had exorcised the house of anything that was not nailed down – and even some items that were. Every light bulb in the house had been taken. The curtains were gone. The mirror – which had been screwed to the bathroom wall – had been removed. Even the toilet roll holder had mysteriously disappeared.

We experienced the coupe de grace when discovering that an entire fitted closet had been completely dismantled and removed leaving a large untidy hole in the carpet where it had previously resided. Angered by this theft, we immediately contacted our Auctioneer who informed us that pursuit of our newly purchased accoutrements would be in vain. Such 'theft' was common in the early 1980's for a simple reason: many people could not afford replacements and took such luxuries with them to their next place of residence.

I had learned a hard lesson, one that I remember to this day. Since our first home purchase we have moved four times. When signing contracts, we now insist that all items being sold with the house are line-itemed in the contract. Even small items such as toilet roll holders.

And so it was that we moved into our 'new' seventy-year-old Terraced Home. It was only then that I truly discovered how different living in Ireland would be for me, and how much of a gap I would have to bridge between the culture of my birth and the culture in which I now chose to live.

A Survivor's Guide to Living in Ireland

Back in the early 1980's many Irish people still heated their houses with coal fires. Some homes were heated with natural gas or 'modern' central heating, and many others were lucky enough to have solid fuel central heating, meaning that the main fire in the house heated a central water cylinder that then transported said heated water into a variety of clanking radiators. In mid-winter these managed to keep the room temperature of this type of centrally heated house warm and toasty.

Our terraced home didn't come with such luxuries and certainly was not in possession of central heating. Consequently, and come wintertime, we simply froze. Often, I would get up on a winter's morning and scrape the ice away from the bedroom window in order to see what the day might be like. This was much different to my boyhood days in wintry Chicago when all I would have to do was turn up the thermostat and the king-sized forced air heater would kick out enough warmth to make me believe that I was in Hawaii. In Ireland my wife or I would get up early, clean the fireplace of its bucket full of ash from the previous day's heating, and pile as much coal as we could within, then huddle over it, praying for a quick dispensation of much needed warmth. We were not alone, of course, because a large minority of the Irish population had to do the same thing. No wonder many of us had such high incidence of asthma, chest infection, and the general feeling that we were going to die come the winter.

While we possessed a refrigerator it wasn't capable of making ice (not that anyone without central heating would ever want ice). Our toilet facilities, such as they were, resided down a short hallway on the ground floor. Neither the hallway nor the bathroom were insulated which meant that in the winter we all literally froze our ass's off when making the call to nature.

Accessing hot water was an experience in patience. We could make hot water in any one of three ways. The first was the back-boiler: the stamp-sized coal fireplace – our only source of heat – came complete with this so-called 'back-boiler', a system that supposedly turned cold water into hot. This gizmo, which was hidden behind a large plate of steel immediately behind the fireplace, contained assorted pipes filled with water. Upon lighting the fire the steel plate came into contact with the flames. The steel heated the pipes that in turn heated the water. The water rose through the series of pipes and was finally disgorged into an abysmally small copper tank that was hidden somewhere deep within the kitchen.

The problem was that to make hot water in this fashion we had to keep the fire going twenty-four hours a day. At six pounds in Irish money – about eight euro – for a bag of coal, a large sum of cash in those days, this prospect was not very likely. Too, the copper tank seemed to contain only enough hot water for approximately one half of one bath. Taking a lukewarm bath in the middle of February is not my idea of fun. Try it sometime. You'll come out wondering at the strange bluish colour of your extremities.

We did, by the way, have a 'shower'. We did not, of course, have a separate shower cubicle the likes of which my parents had in the United States and which I borrowed as a teenager in order to soak myself for half a day, then to come out looking like a steamed prune. The shower in our terraced house in Navan was a simple rubber tube that we could connect with some difficulty to the spout in the bath. A ridiculous spray unit was glued to the other end of the tube. The tube wasn't long enough to allow us to stand up, so instead we had to sit down in the bath.

In winter, and should I desire to put myself through torture, I would sit in the ice-cold tub at which point my buttocks would become firmly attached requiring immediate rescue by my wife. In that the house had the water pressure of a squirt gun, the resultant dribble from the ineptly engineered spray unit might result in the application of mere ounces of water, not enough to engender even the slightest excitement from a bar of soap.

For this reason I rarely took a shower.

But back to the hot water: The second option was to turn on what was euphemistically called 'The Geezer'. This was an absolutely ancient, ugly as hell contraption that was bolted onto the wall just above the bath. It ran on electricity. This 'Geezer' was comprised of a copper tank filled with water. Electricity, which at the time seemed to cost more per kilowatt-hour than plane fare to Hong Kong, was applied at which point the water would heat up and the knowing bather would then open a stubborn tap, spilling the hot contents into the bath. Here, the problem was possible electrocution. Consequently, I avoided use of The Geezer whenever possible.

The third option was the jug kettle. When all else failed we boiled up one small kettle after another, transported these in shifts from kitchen to bathroom, and poured the contents into the bath. In that our kettle only held one litre of water it took quite a few kettles and much boiling to fill the tub. Of course, by the time we had completed this mission the bathwater had again turned lukewarm so we were as well to light the fire and wait for the back-boiler to rattle, hiss, and otherwise make us aware that hot water was on its way. The jug kettle option, however, also allowed me to make a cup of tea for my good wife at the same time, so wasn't a bad option depending on the state of our relationship.

The outcome of all of this was that we managed to get quite dirty for a few months, until I had acquired enough cash through incredibly hard toil to upgrade the hot water facilities. In the meantime the baby got her bath in the kitchen sink. But we all survived, nonetheless.

As to the house itself, and as partially described above, it was an old two bedroom council house made prettier by a carpet of small white flowers which I soon discovered to be a variety of local weed, that poked through the unkempt front garden. I now remember that upon first seeing the house I really did think that it looked quite 'quaint', a reaction that should have set off all sorts of internal alarm bells, but which at the time only made me feel cosy. It sat in the middle of a row of such houses and was built completely of poured concrete. The walls were at least twelve inches thick. While it was never going to fall down, putting up a picture or moving an electrical socket meant heavy excavation work and a heightening of blood pressure as I drilled through the heavy concrete walls, choking on early twentieth century cement dust that did its best to cover anything – including the baby – in a shroud of white.

The rooms were so small that had I tried swinging the proverbial cat I would have caused immediate decapitation. This version of reality did not, of course, match the dreams that I had imagined during my ruminations over a pint at the local. Instead, we lived in a turn of the century dwelling that felt like living in some sort of industrial site and that allowed us to have a bath only when we could get the hot water to work. In short, I despised the place.

But I must stress that those feelings of squalor have long since left me. It took me years to understand why I reacted to that house like I did, but the answer was simple. I was a spoiled American who had grown used to the 'finer' things in life. Despite my best efforts not to, I was being dragged kicking and screaming through the process of adjusting to a new culture, and a new way of living and looking at things.

Back in 1982, and while there were wealthy people around who possessed all of the accoutrements of being wealthy, we didn't have much and neither did many of the people whom we knew. But in hindsight, I marvel at a simple realisation: none of these people – people who I considered 'poor' along with myself – missed anything simply because no one had anything either. Instead, they worked day-to-day and managed to get by. And not only that, but they were happy and content with their lot.

For instance, my mother-in-law lived in a similar house to our own just down the road for most of her seventy-five years. In that structure, which could have easily fitted into my parents' backyard, she and her husband made a loving home and Kathleen raised eight children including my wife, Bernie. Her memories of living there are not of hardship but rather of great fun and a warmth of living that is sometimes difficult to find in modern Ireland, or come to think of it, almost anywhere else anymore.

Now, I look back on those early days with a certain fondness and I'm glad that I went through the experience. If I had stayed in America I'm not certain that I would ever have been as broke, and the experience has allowed me to value what I have today. And looking back I now see what I couldn't see at the time: we never had to lock our front door because crime was almost non-existent. We relied on our neighbours in times of difficulty much as they relied on us. We shared what little we had with each other because that was the way of things. In short, we had become a part of the local 'tribe', and tribe members take care of each other.

I had trouble living in our cold little home simply because I was used to instant hot water, nuclear-powered central heating, rooms big enough to house entire villages, and a bathroom that

A Survivor's Guide to Living in Ireland

wouldn't cause personal injury every time I went to dispose of yesterday's lunch.

Over the past twenty-some years, however, things in Ireland have changed dramatically, some for the better, some for the worse.

Navan can now be a quite pleasant place to live, thank you very much. With the coming prosperity of the country, our town has managed to benefit substantially. What with the expansion of Dublin over twenty thousand people have moved into the place, turning the town on its head and creating some amazing opportunities.

The shopping centre has been expanded and refurbished in order to accommodate the swelling crowds. Older shops have been repainted and entire new retail sections of Navan have been built, selling everything from apples to exercise equipment.

We no longer have to rely on one Chinese restaurant. Now, we have a choice of anything from Thai food to the best Italian fare. Streets have been torn up and resurfaced; broken footpaths replaced by lovely brick walks that glisten prettily in the soft rains.

The River Boyne, which flows through the town and which had heretofore been thought of as nothing more than an amenity for local fishermen, has been upgraded with lovely walkways along its historic banks. Many are the days that I spend whiling away my time by walking beneath the beautiful archways created by oak trees and yew, the sun-dappled river talking to me in hushed conversation.

And though I eventually moved away from it, even my old terraced house has seen the benefit of new windows and a coat of paint.

When I first arrived in Navan, and for a number of years, it is true to say that I absolutely hated living here. The gap between cultures – between how I was raised and what I was used to, and what I found here and how I had to adapt – proved incredibly difficult. Hell, when I first moved to Ireland I couldn't even buy peanut butter.

But things have changed. The country has moved on. No longer are immigrants from the States, Europe or elsewhere confronted by a struggling economy that can bring thoughts of suicide to a confused and dangerously homesick mind. The phones work. Houses are heated properly. Everyone has a car, sometimes two, sometimes three. Most of us can afford to take expensive holidays. In short, Ireland is no longer a poverty-stricken nation. And though it is not America or mainland Europe and takes some getting used to, it offers many of the amenities that the U.S. doesn't seem to have anymore, such as a joy of living and a recognition of personal relationships that seems, sadly enough, to have grown unpopular back home. That, and a whole lot more.

But Navan, as with the rest of the country, has lost something in the transition. Though its streets are clean they are clogged with the traffic of a successful economy. Today, we keep our doors locked because we are concerned about vandals and theft. While neighbours still look after each other, we don't have as much time to chat or get to know each other simply because we are all working so very hard. And though my family now lives in a modern house with modern plumbing and all of the hot water we could ever need, that old terraced house now brings to mind the realisation that I not only survived – despite my American-ness – but have also managed to prosper in this country.

For years I thought of grabbing my family and escaping from this country back to the land of my birth. But just as the country has changed, so too have I. I've now discovered that I'm glad that I stayed. I survived the challenge. Now, I realise that I've earned the right to stay here even longer.

As the years have passed I have gradually come to regard Ireland as my home.

Guideline Five
How to Buy a Piece of Irish Heaven for Yourself

Chicago, Illinois   *August 14, 1983*

Dear Tom,

I am astonished that you have taken the trouble to write in order to give me advice that you know I could not possibly follow. You know very well that I would never be interested in living in Ireland, no matter how beautiful it is or how affordable the housing.

I think that there is the distinct possibility that you have been kidnapped by a cult and have become brainwashed into their nefarious ways. It could well be that you require the help of a psychiatrist.

Do please struggle against their methods! You are too well loved to become a lost soul in that land of bogs and constant rain. For me, the American Dream is sacrosanct. I will never succumb to a land hallmarked by tales of non-existent Leprechauns.

I continue to care for you but I would never willingly move to Ireland. Thank you anyway for the invitation.

Ronald

Location, location, location. Isn't that what the property guru's always tell you? It's no different in Ireland. The question, of course, is what kind of location you'd prefer.

If you choose, like I did, to nay-say the nay-sayers and to come here in pursuit of your own small corner of the Irish dream, you have a great deal to consider. For instance, where-oh-where in this wonderful country would you prefer to make your home? Every location in this country – as with many other nations or geographies – has something different to offer.

Are you interested in living in a City Centre? You can choose from the vibrancy of any of Ireland's major cities and towns. Dublin, Waterford, Cork, Galway, Wexford, Athlone, Belfast…each has something different and unique to give to the erstwhile seeker-after-Ireland.

Like the rest of Ireland, all major cities and towns have benefited from a significant facelift. Dublin, for instance, has undergone substantial redevelopment over the past ten years. When I first arrived on these shores, many of the beautiful Georgian houses that hallmarked the city centre were in danger of falling down from lack of maintenance, and the River Liffey was blighted by an assortment of rotting tenements and ancient warehouses that lined its famous banks.

But significant investment by the European Union and the Irish government, the vibrancy of the local economy, together with an upsurge in incomes, has provided the country with an unprecedented level of prosperity. The infrastructure of Dublin has benefited from this. Starting in the mid-1990's, the city has been hallmarked by dozens of construction cranes dotting the cityscape. Many of the nineteenth century Georgian homes have been gutted and completely refurbished while maintaining their lofty ceilings and unique external fascia's. Entire Georgian office blocks running along the River Liffey were completely redeveloped.

New apartment blocks were constructed: an entire community of shops, pubs, arts centres, offices and flats, running along the south side of the Liffey, was recreated in the Temple Bar area. To the north of the River, and in addition to the development of the Irish Financial Services Centre, the area has been bolstered by the construction of river front walkways, small shops and cafes, new bridges that have been thrown over the River, and any number of street-side apartments.

On O'Connell Street, at the heart of Dublin, we even have a new piece of architecture to argue over. The Spire – a piece of exquisite aluminium – now thrusts into the skies above the city like a New Age toothpick. It replaces Nelson's Pillar, a throwback to English colonialism and a past tribute to the famous English Admiral. Erected in 1808, three years after the naval commander's death, it was finally blown up on March 8, 1966 by IRA sympathisers who believed that a memorial to the victor of the Battle of Trafalgar was entirely inappropriate rising, as it did, to its lofty height above the Irish Republic's bustling capital. For years, the Irish argued over a suitable replacement. Finally, and after much to-ing and fro-ing, the powers that be finally decided on The Spire. Though this contemporary structure was expensive and many argue that the money could have been better spent on a new hospital wing or decreasing the price of petrol, I think that it's pretty and certainly illustrates the potential of this proud country and the future that it is energetically pursuing.

Taking a stroll through Dublin is a unique experience. The Abbey Theatre, the Gate Theatre, shopping along Grafton Street, a visit to local cafes for afternoon tea and scones – all are within walking distance. To live in Dublin is to share some of the experiences of the life of James Joyce. And though Dublin is now a modern place complete with modern architecture, the city planners have managed to retain the old fascia and the sense of charm and history that had until recently been lost beneath the grime of an economically troubled period.

Smaller cities throughout the country have also benefited from a significant polish during the exceptional years of the Celtic Tiger. Pick a city and you will inevitably find your own special mix of old world charm and modern infrastructure.

Wexford with its narrow streets and pleasant harbour, Waterford and its quick access to overseas ferries and the rest of Europe, Cork and its pleasing shopping streets and intimate pubs, and the surging city of Galway, one of Ireland's smallest cities and oldest, renowned for its world-class University, seafood, singsong and Irish craic.

If city life doesn't appeal to you, look to country living. Ireland's Midlands (find Portlaoise or Athlone on the map and you're looking at the Midlands) offer a quiet life devoid of crowds, smog and stress. In their search for a location, most people never think to even look to the Midlands. But much of it is pretty. A millennia ago, the countryside was levelled by the glacial flows of the Ice Age. These icy protuberances were not only responsible for destroying a countryside full of leafy Irish oak forests (which have since become bogs and which the Irish harvest as peat to burn as winter fuel) but also levelled everything else in their path. What remains – mostly, anyway – is as flat as a pancake. But through the Midlands courses the River Shannon and along its waterway reside both some wonderful towns and beautiful lakes.

If seaside locations appeal, take your time about selecting a desired place of beauty. Ireland's coastline – from west to east, north to south – undergoes a tremendous change of character within even the shortest of distances. The East coast along the Irish Sea offers plenty of sandy beaches and a reasonably temperate climate. Go south to County Cork and you'll find pleasant inlets and somewhat warmer days.

As you move up the Southwest coast past County Kerry and toward Limerick and Galway, the coastline becomes tougher and more unforgiving. High cliffs catch the surging ocean, tossing sea spray skyward, while north of Galway – up in County Donegal – rest some of the best beaches and purest waters anywhere, rivalling the world's better known locations for their un-surpassing beauty.

If you fancy sea life, the West coast also offers some spectacular aquatic encounters due to the close proximity of the Gulf Stream. Dolphins, porpoise, whales, sharks, and some of the best diving in Europe are available anywhere up and down the West coast of Ireland. If you can brave the cold of the Atlantic, you'll be in for a unique diving experience that you'll not soon forget.

Or drive north from Dublin and venture into Counties Cavan and Monaghan. Here, the countryside undulates in a series of hills and valleys and small lakes and ponds dot the place. Property prices in these counties remain reasonable and a prospective purchaser would be remiss if they did not at least investigate the area. For instance, new detached four bedroom houses are selling for just over two hundred thousand euro (about two hundred and fifty thousand U.S. dollars): a good bargain compared to the prices that one now finds in Dublin, a drive of only two hours south of that pristine region.

My suggestion? Visit the country and stay awhile before choosing a location. For Heaven's sake, don't do what I did and make a location decision without the benefit of seeing what was available in the rest of the country. For such a small island, Ireland has an incredible choice on offer. Take in its beauty before making up your mind.

Choosing the Right Estate Agent

Ireland has any number of real estate agencies. A few of the biggest include Gunnes, Douglas Newman Good, Hamilton Osborne King, and Sherry Fitzgerald. These are national agencies, but many larger towns and all cities will also have their own local auctioneers.

My gut assessment is that the smaller and more intimate the agency, the better their knowledge of the local area and what is on offer. While the local agents may not have a national scope, their attitude seems to be friendlier and one that is determined to satisfy all parties, both the buyer and the seller. They will go to almost any length to close a deal that is satisfactory to everyone.

National estate agents, on the other hand and by their very nature, offer a network of offices throughout the country that can provide a one-stop-shop facility to those of you interested in searching out properties both near and far.

If you have a reasonable idea of the location that you're interested in, try a local auctioneer. If, on the other hand, you don't yet have a good knowledge of the country, then try the national agents.

In most cases, the agents that I've worked with have been both highly professional and honest. But I've heard the war stories of agents who, having spotted the rich accent of a prospective American or European buyer, rub their hands in greed. As with any financial undertaking, my suggestion is that you not only interview a prospective estate agent but also try to get your hands on references.

Unlike the United States and many parts of the rest of the world, and no matter whom you choose, you will soon find that Irish estate agents are not the most motivated folks in the world. In the U.S., it seemed that a real estate agent would drop everything at the first phone call to ferry a prospect from one end of his or her territory to another in the hope of closing a deal.

Here, things operate on a much different timescale. Having made contact with the estate agent of your choice expect things to happen at what can sometimes seem a snail's pace. The estate agent will inevitably have to book a viewing with a seller, and that viewing might be days away. If you're in a rush make it clear that you need adequate attention, and that you wish to see more than one property a day. Also, give the estate agent adequate time to organise multiple viewings for the same day.

New Construction

Currently, Ireland is enjoying a surge in new construction in what seems to be almost every corner of the country. Entire new towns, new communities, and new estates are popping up like mushrooms in a damp field.

Building contractors are catering for all financial markets, building everything from city centre one bedroom apartments, to estates filled with ubiquitous semi-detached housing, to more salubrious estates featuring houses with large living areas, broadband wiring, multiple bedrooms with en suites (which are separate bathrooms attached to the bedrooms, e.g. a Master Bath), under floor heating, huge outdoor gardens, and often coming completely furnished down to the tiniest inessentials. Most construction here is composed of the concrete breezeblock type, but non-traditional methods including wooden frames and log cabin kits are also making an appearance.

Heating and insulation methods are critical in this land of cold and damp and many builders have bettered their specifications with uPVC double pane windows, hi-spec insulation, and in-floor heating methods. Heating types vary throughout the country: all new houses incorporate central heating as standard. Depending on the home's location, energy sources can include oil heating, natural gas, or solid fuel (coal fired).

Natural gas is by far the least expensive and most trouble-free of all heating options. It certainly beats cleaning out the soot from a central fire every day. Unfortunately, natural gas is not available in many parts of the country, which is an appalling state of affairs especially considering that any number of international oil companies have found incredible reserves of this resource off the coasts of Ireland. However, the government – through its semi-State company Bord Gais – is currently doing what it can to bring this economic fuel to the rest of the country.

Ask your estate agent about availability of natural gas in your area.

A Survivor's Guide to Living in Ireland

And a Word About Prices

I have good news and bad news about house prices in this country. When I first came here Ireland was an incredibly inexpensive place in which to buy a home. Housing was cheap by American and European standards and even though I struggled to buy a house here, my circumstances were due to the fact that I arrived in this country almost penniless. Back then, an immigrant with a bit of cash in his or her wallet could buy a modest two-bedroom dwelling for less than twenty thousand U.S. dollars. An abandoned cottage could be had for less than fifteen thousand.

I even heard tell of a fifteenth century castle going for less than the price of a suburban tract home in the San Francisco Bay area.

Unfortunately, all of that has changed.

Ireland is no longer a banana republic. As a member of the European Union this country has prospered at an incredible rate. On a per capita basis Ireland is one of the richest countries in the EU, recently passing out both England and Germany. It is also the most expensive, last year beating out Finland for that dubious honour.

Ireland also possesses one of the youngest populations in Europe. And all of those young people seem to want to get a leg up on the property ladder.

Combine these factors with a shortage in supply of new housing (despite the swaths of new construction dotting the country) and every economist will point out one inevitable consequence: housing is bound to get more expensive. And it has.

I've already mentioned my experience of purchasing a property here in 1982. Let me tell you another story that illustrates the frightening increase in property values in Ireland since that time.

In 1992 my wife and I made another purchase, this time moving to a modest four bedroom semi-detached home located yet again in Navan. At the time, the town was still considered to be a part of the hinterland despite its location only thirty miles up the road from Dublin. In that year, we bought our house for a mere forty-three thousand Irish pounds, or approximately sixty thousand U.S. dollars.

Then a funny thing happened. The global economy started to grow like mad, propelled by the advent of new technologies.

Starting in 1995, things in Ireland went crazy. All of a sudden everyone was talking about stock options rather than the lowly state of their financial affairs.

The country grew rich. With money in their pockets – an exciting new experience for many – people rushed out and bought things: BMW's, new computers, designer make up and clothing, luxury watches, jacuzzi's, mobile telephones – everyone seemed determined to make up for a history of poverty with the sudden urge to buy. And as I watched, what heretofore had been a country on the last rung of the economic ladder quickly turned into one of the most prosperous countries in the world.

For over five years, until the Internet bubble floated into history, the Irish Gross National Product grew at double-digit figures. Ireland seemed to set record after record: it exported more computer software than any other country in the world. Its unemployment – approaching a disastrous twenty percent when I first ventured to this wonderful part of the world – fell at an unprecedented rate to virtually nil in 2002. The country flexed its entrepreneurial skills and more new companies were set up over that period of time than at any other time in its history.

Awash with cash, awash with demand, awash with a new (and perhaps disjointed) perception of themselves, Ireland's citizens bought and bought and bought. And one of their most sought-after purchases was a new house. Consequently, the housing market took off like a rocket-powered aircraft attempting to set a new altitude record.

Sitting in our little semi-detached home, my wife and I watched with ever-growing astonishment as the economy bubbled and brewed and began to hiss like a teakettle. Navan quickly became a bedroom community as Dublin people attempted to find themselves a little corner of the Irish dream and exited the city in search for more affordable accommodation. Our neighbours began selling up, making profits that were unheard of even a few years before.

And in 1999 we decided to cash in.

We put our modest house on the market. We received an initial offer of one hundred and ten thousand Irish pounds. We couldn't believe it. Our estate agent, an intelligent woman and wise to the new market conditions, told us to wait. Two other bidders entered the fray. The price moved to one fifteen. Then one-twenty. Finally on one bright April day, when my conscience could take no more, we asked the two bidders who remained engaged in a battle that I feared might lead to their financial ruination to submit a sealed envelope with their final offers.

The winning bid? *One hundred and twenty-five thousand and one pounds.* Almost three times what we had paid for it a mere seven years earlier. I remind you that the new owner paid this plush amount – and considered it a bargain – for a house of only thirteen hundred square feet, four small bedrooms, and one bathroom. The amount paid then was equivalent to approximately one hundred and fifty thousand U.S. dollars. For the same amount, and at that time, I could have purchased a twenty five hundred square foot home in Tampa with a swimming pool. Amazing.

It was the best investment that we had ever made. And it was all due to timing.

Since then, Ireland's population has become transfixed with the price of property. Even though the world economy has cooled following 9/11, Ireland's property market is as buoyant as ever. Mortgage interest rates – now approximately four percent for a twenty year fixed mortgage – are part of the reason for the stratospheric increase in prices. But Ireland's ever increasing population, its young citizens clamouring for a house of their own, and a continuing shortage of property has meant that houses of all types and located almost anywhere in the country are continuing to appreciate at between five and ten percent per annum.

Dublin, unfortunately, is now almost untouchably unaffordable to the regular purchaser. Recently, a block of single bedroom apartments of no more than nine hundred square feet came on the market. Located in the City Centre, they went for approximately four hundred thousand euro a-piece! What's amazing is the fact that they were snapped up almost instantly.

The Irish have become so crazy to purchase a house that they'll even buy off the plans, before construction has begun.

Rentals and leaseholds have also followed the trend. Rental prices for even a tiny apartment in Dublin are comparable to renting a similar property in Manhattan. Only you can't get a decent hotdog in Dublin.

The country has gone mad.

So the bad news is this: Irish property prices aren't what they used to be. It's now expensive to purchase even a modest dwelling. 'Expensive', of course, is relative. What's inexpensive to you might not be to another person. But, as far as I'm concerned, things are expensive for *me* let me tell you.

But there is good news. An investment in an Irish property is undoubtedly one of the best investments that you'll ever make. Consider this: when my wife and I sold our semi-detached four bedroom home, we purchased a brand new twenty-two hundred square foot house – with three centrally heated bathrooms, thank God – right up the street (I'll never get out of Navan, it seems). At the time, we paid one hundred and seventy two thousand Irish pounds for it, which equates (in new currency) to two hundred and eighteen thousand euro, or over two hundred and seventy thousand U.S. dollar.

My friendly auctioneer reliably tells me that my house now carries a value of over three hundred and seventy thousand euro. In that we've lived at the new house almost six years now that works out to an appreciation of over twenty-five thousand euro each and every year of our ownership.

Investing in the Irish property market has to date carried much less risk than the stock market, bonds, or other financial instruments. And it's certainly better than the miserable one percent interest or so available on any savings you might have in a bank account. Economists are currently projecting that – unless worldwide economic disaster strikes or interest rates move suddenly skyward – the upward movement in Irish property values will continue, albeit at a slower and more controlled pace.

The other piece of good news is the fact that bargains – comparably speaking, of course – still exist in Ireland if you're willing to stay away from city centres. The inland counties of Cavan, Monahan and Leitrim still offer exceptional value for even larger homes. For instance, just south of Cavan Town, in the small village of Cootehill, a new four-bedroom semi-detached home is on offer for just shy of one hundred and thirty eight thousand euro. Another listing, this time for a renovated two-storey home comprising four bedrooms is going for one hundred and thirty five thousand.

And if you're willing to look around, you can still find reasonably priced properties with seaside and country amenities. In Caherciveen, County Kerry a three-bedroom cottage with views of the Bay is on offer for just shy of two hundred thousand euro, while a four bedroom home on an inland location is going for one hundred and eighty four thousand euro.

Unfortunately, however, the days of the run-down cottage in need of refurbishment and available for a wink and a nod are long dead. Get used to it. Ireland has become part of the twenty-first century. And so have its property prices.

Guideline Six
Ireland is Expensive. Or Is It?

Chicago, Illinois   *January 15, 1984*

Dear Tom,

I am concerned that you have not written to me since my last communication. However, your Mother assures me that you are safe.

I thought that you would appreciate the fact that we have just finished an absolutely wonderful, obnoxiously materialistic Christmas season. Robert came home from Peru, and we forgave him by giving him his own brand new Firebird complete with eight track player and some tapes by groups of strangely named birds.

Helen received her own multi-functional vacuum cleaner, and I let Santa treat me somewhat extravagantly to a complete wine cellar filled with assorted bins of Cabernet Sauvignon.

But enough of us. How was your Christmas? I do hope that you are enjoying your newfound poverty. I suspect that you have been surprised at your lack of employable skills in a country renowned only for its unemployment. I am also shocked that you have managed to survive for as long as you have in that country. I suspect that you miss the comforts of America.

Do come home at once!

Yours,

Ronald

When I received Ronald's positively infuriating letter I remember wanting to tear it up and throw it into the smouldering coal fire. Instead I folded it neatly thinking that I'd keep it to remind myself of my days of poverty. Then, determined to make myself more miserable, I emptied my pockets and discovered that I had exactly seventy-two pence on me and realised that this fortune would have to do until the next payday.

In the meantime we were going to have to eat. A neat trick back then, because in those days of the early 1980's Ireland was expensive.

In fact, it can seem to be as expensive now as it was in 1982 if not more so. If you're planning on immigrating to Ireland I strongly recommend that the first thing you do is run out and rob Fort Knox before boarding the airplane. Even if you are crazy enough to imagine yourself living here as a New Age Hippie, hoping to squat in some field with only a tent over your head, do remember please that even the simple things in Irish life can set you back plenty.

Back in 1982, my own personal circumstances – and those of the entire country – were tough enough. My first job here was working as a salesman for an industrial weighing company, travelling the width and breadth of Ireland trying to sell worthless bits of metal to farmers' cooperatives and tight-fisted Irish business people at the princely take home pay of five hundred quid a month. Ireland didn't only seem expensive to me, it was.

I was not alone. The average industrial wage at that point was just over one hundred pounds a week. Each payday, everyone ran home to rip open their pay packets, spilled its contents on the kitchen table, and prayed that somehow they'd manage to get through to the next week. At least that's what we did.

Out of our monthly earnings, Bernie and I had to pay for:

Mortgage	£117 per month
Food	£100 per month
Coal	£ 30 per month
College Loan	£ 30 per month
Petrol	£100 per month
Car Insurance/Taxes	£ 50 per month
Electricity	£ 25 per month
Clothing	£ 20 per month
Miscellaneous	£ 20 per month
Total	£492 per month

A Survivor's Guide to Living in Ireland

This left us eight quid per month with which to do exactly as we pleased. With this extravagant sum, we could either: purchase approximately fourteen pints of Guinness, go to the chipper four times, buy a few packs of cigarettes each, or otherwise go entirely mad with our vast fortune. We could, of course, have put this into our savings but I had entirely given up the prospects of retiring any time before my one-hundredth birthday. Back home, I had always tried to save ten percent of my salary. Having gone to the bank I would hold up my bankbook in satisfaction, hoping that those pennies would someday give birth to an outrageous fortune. In Ireland, however, and considering our circumstances, saving would have to wait and the entire concept of being rich, or even financially comfortable, became only a fading dream.

We never considered extravagances like a foreign holiday or the purchase of a new car. That kind of thinking was considered reckless and ill conceived. Besides, what would we do with a new car? We couldn't have afforded the insurance.

Many other people in the country lived like this as well. Very few of us owned cars and almost no one went out for a four-course meal in a fancy restaurant or hotel except on those rare occasions such as weddings, Confirmations, or funerals. On those special moments everyone threw caution to the wind, borrowed a tidy sum from the local credit union, feasted as if there was no tomorrow, and woke up petrified the next day knowing, as they did, that they had signed a slip of paper promising that they would pay back the debt for the rest of the year at a staggering five pounds per week. Unfortunately, those were pounds that few of us could afford.

When I stepped off the plane, with very little cash available to ward off starvation, I hadn't thought about such trivialities as being able to afford to eat every day. The thought never even occurred to me. Based on what I had seen in *The Quiet Man*, and those rousing scenes of large plates of boiled potatoes being thrown at equally large farmhands, I assumed that the country was awash in good fortune and I imagined that life in Ireland would be at least affordable if not luxurious.

I was wrong.

The first shock that I received was my purchase of a fourteen-inch colour television set. When Bernie and I lived in America we had bought a similar set but because the U.S. operates on 120 volts while the rest of the world seems to run on 240 volts the damned thing wouldn't work in Ireland. It's also a fact that television signals are transmitted and received differently in Ireland (PAL in Europe, NTSC in the United States), and therefore our U.S. television would only show snow if we had brought it along. So we gave it to my sister and knew that we would have to buy a new one once we had successfully planted our feet in our new home.

I had bought the old set in a high quality shop for exactly $249.99, on sale because it was an old model, but a good make despite that fact.

Having moved into our terraced council house previously mentioned I knew that the next step to permanent residence in the country was the purchase of our own television. I walked down the pathways, looking like a drunk as I tried to avoid the broken bits of concrete, and into town. There, I entered Navan's only electrical appliance shop, a run down establishment that looked as if it had barely survived British occupation, with optimism in my heart.

I, the sophisticated American, was going to take the Irish retail establishment by storm and strike a bargain.

The salesman on the shop floor, surrounded by broken televisions, telephones, old radios, and the other flotsam of his trade, looked up from his cashbook and tried to engage me with his best 'I'm a fellow that you can trust' look as I approached.

'Good morning, my friend. And it's a wonderful day, isn't it, if the rain would stay off.' I knew that he was trying to soften me up because I had just walked through a virtual downpour and he was only making small talk. Pleasantries aside, he quickly got down to business. 'And what can I do to help you? A radio perhaps to listen to the Irish football?'

'I'd like to buy a TV,' I stated firmly.

'Now would that be a used TV or a new TV?' he asked. 'Black and white or colour? With or without one of the new remote control units?'

A used television? For me? Not on your life. I thought about it for maybe two seconds and decided to go the whole hog. 'New, colour...,' then, thinking of the lowly state of our savings account, '...but maybe leave out the remote.'

'Well, you've won the Irish Sweeps, haven't you? And isn't that marvellous!' He gazed at me as if he'd found a recently butchered fatted calf, then reached up toward a tangled mass of dusty catalogues on a shelf above his head, pulled out a book that looked as if it had never been touched, and plopped it on the counter in front of me.

Eagerly, sensing a large profit, he thumbed through its pages. He found what he was looking for and turned the page toward me. A fairly standard television stared back. It looked ordinary enough. It was black. It had a screen. It had little push-button gadgets and rabbit ear aerials for those of us that didn't have cable.

Cable in Ireland was nonexistent in those days, so the rabbit ears were just fine.

'Now this will do the job for you,' he said. 'Yours for only four hundred and thirty nine pounds, fifty pence, and quite a bargain at that.'

Four hundred and thirty-nine pounds! For a fourteen-inch colour television without remote, one almost the same as the one I had bought less than a year ago for a couple hundred bucks? This was an outrage!

I swallowed hard. 'You're certain about that? I just emigrated here from the States. Twelve months ago I bought exactly the same thing for a just over two hundred dollars. That's only one hundred and fifty pounds or so.' I poked at the photo in front of me. 'And now you're telling me that this thing is going to cost me *six hundred and sixty dollars?*'

'That, as they say, is the price of living in Ireland.' He smiled sweetly, probably knowing that I was going to have to buy it from him or spend the rest of my days staring at a blank wall. 'Well, you could always do the H.P. You pay a fiver a week for five years and it's yours. That's what most people do.'

Back in the old days of the 1980's, many Irish citizens purchased larger capital investments – such as a twelve inch television – on the HP. Higher Purchase was, I have since learned, a despicable financing arrangement backed by most retailers that cost the poor Irish consumer over double the already outrageously inflated price of the product in question. Retailers became rich on such gimmicks while their fellow townspeople simply became poorer. I was determined to avoid H.P at all costs. I calculated quickly. At a fiver a week for five years, purchasing this un-ornate television with no remote control so that I could watch the latest episode of *Dallas* was going to set me back thirteen hundred quid. Back home and for the same price I could have bought an entire entertainment system complete with Dolby surround-sound, with the *Beatles* greatest hits thrown in for the hell of it.

No thank you.

'Why the hell is it so damned expensive?' I demanded to know. Surely this guy was trying to rip off an innocent American. I wanted to know why.

'It's the VAT, you see. The government has us there, now don't they?' he stated, thereby blaming the Irish government for everything. In some ways he was, of course, correct. As previously mentioned, the Irish government, as well as most governments in Europe, tax everything that moves and most of the stuff that doesn't. Unlike U.S. state tax, where the five or seven percent tax is added onto the product price as a separate line item, VAT is always included in the price so that the poor consumer must calculate this outrageous rip-off mentally.

The Irish government also taxes everything else that you can possibly think of and at preposterously burdensome levels: some food items, drink, petrol, houses, land, animals, cars, cigarettes, alcohol, restaurant meals, plastic bags, hay, flowers, aircraft landings, new construction, old construction, and tickets to the next U2 concert. Over seventy percent of every gallon of petrol goes to tax. Almost half of any new car purchase ends up in government coffers.

The average working stiff actually ends up with just under fifty percent of his or her income to buy things with. The rest goes to the government.

In the case of the television I was paying the Irish government an astonishing £74.45 for the honour of making the purchase. Every now and then some jarhead U.S. Congressman suggests the idea of VAT. Recently, for instance, I noticed in a Tampa, Florida newspaper a small article that quoted a number of U.S. officials, including the Chairman of the Federal Reserve, saying that they firmly believed that a new consumption tax would be a good thing for America. If they haven't told you, and I doubt that they have, a consumption tax is the same thing as VAT. These idiot politicians and bureaucrats believe – and rightly so – that this tax would be akin to printing money and would finance all sorts of new government salaries, perks, and other useless line items. I shudder to think about it. My advice to the American taxpayer: any member of Congress who so much as utters the word 'VAT' (or 'consumption tax' for that matter) should be voted out of office as quickly as humanly possible. VAT has to be one of the most unfair, outrageous, and inflationary taxes around.

But back to the TV: the shop proprietor gazed at me with his perfectly innocent eyes and said: 'Well, you could always buy a used one.'

Needless to say I purchased the new television. Then, for my trouble, I had to carry the damned thing all the way home. However, it's fair to say that for four hundred, thirty-nine pounds, fifty pence it did after all turn out to be good value. After all of these years the bloody thing still works.

But there's good news. As mentioned above, things have changed in Ireland. Increased competition, increased production efficiencies, and increased consumer demand have all helped to put downward pressure on the prices for many Irish goods. Now, you can buy a brand new 14 inch colour television with remote control for as little as one hundred and fifty euro! Other electrical items have also declined dramatically in price. Everything from electric kettles to hairdryers, washing machines to electric toothbrushes, digital cameras to Personal Computers cost much less than they did in the first days of my Irish residency. While we still pay more than most U.S. and European consumers for comparable electrical goods, I often discover that Irish prices for brown and white goods approach those of many other retailers, even when purchased in the Wal-Marts of this world.

Other consumer items have also fallen in real terms: air travel, for instance, has dropped substantially due to increased competition. An example: in 1982 a round-trip flight to London (only just over an hour by air from Dublin) could be had for the staggering sum of well over two hundred Irish pounds (approximately two hundred and fifty euro). That same flight can now cost as little as fifty euro. Flights to the United States, Continental Europe, and many other parts of the world have also declined significantly due in most part to increasing competition among the world's airline carriers. For instance, I recently flew to Berlin. The cost? Just over one hundred euro.

Package holidays (two weeks to Spain, Greece, France, or Portugal for instance) have also fallen dramatically. A place in the sun for two weeks for you and your family, staying in a lovely bolthole like the Algarve in Portugal, will only set you back a few thousand euro, and that's all inclusive. Would you rather plan your own Continental holiday? Then do what many people do and avail of the substantial savings to be found on the World Wide Web. Last year, I took my good wife to Sorrento in Italy. We had a fabulous stay in a hotel that was perched on a cliff, looking for all the world like some sort of monastic enclave, only with hot running water and food that couldn't be beat. The stunning views of Mount Vessuvius didn't hurt, either. I booked the entire holiday over the Internet. The total cost for four wonderful days? A few hundred euro.

Like most places in the world, communication costs in Ireland have also fallen substantially. A phone call to the States from Ireland is now less expensive than a similar call made from the States to this country. The same is true for telephone calls to Continental Europe: calls to London, Berlin, Paris, Barcelona, and anywhere else I can think of are only a few euro cent a minute. That sure beats the torturous telephone prices that I experienced when I first came to this country. While it's true that we continue to call the country 'Rip Off Ireland', it is also true that due to increased competition and demand, prices on many items have actually fallen and often by substantial amounts.

But while some things have come down in price, other items here remain extortionately high when compared to the U.S., England, or mainland Europe. The cost of staying in a hotel, the price of taking your love out for a good meal and a bottle of palatable wine, the ridiculous expense of purchasing simple treats such as a gas barbeque – all of these can set you back plenty when compared to many other countries. Unfortunately, Ireland continues to be an expensive place in which to set up shop. To fight back, you just have to keep your eyes open and search for those good deals.

A Survivor's Guide to Living in Ireland

What's So Expensive About It?

As of this writing, Ireland is now considered to be the most expensive EU country in which to live, outdistancing even the Northern European nations in our drive to discover just how much the Irish wallet can take.

Taxes, as outlined above, continue to drive up prices. As the country has grown richer, employees have sought much needed wage increases and have received them. Then local distributors and manufacturers, keenly aware of the mountain of disposable income now floating through the economy, increased prices which meant that inflation increased and the working masses sought even greater wage hikes. Ireland has become a textbook case of a wage and price spiral. Prices increase, then wages go up, then prices bound ahead even further. Now, discussing the cost of living has become more popular than talking about the prevarications of the weather. And Irish people have always had a great fondness for discussing the weather.

A typical discussion goes like this:

Neighbour: 'Did you hear? The government, damn their souls to hell, is considering putting a tax on water.'
Me: 'What else is new? They've taxed everything else.'
Neighbour: 'But what are we going to do about it? I'm already paying through the nose for my house payment, keeping the family in food, the kids in clothes, and have just about enough money left to keep the car in petrol.'
Me: 'Things could be worse. You could lose your job.'
Neighbour: 'Thanks so very much. Now I won't be able to sleep tonight.'

Just like any other culture, the Irish love to bitch and moan about the high cost of living. In many ways, they're right of course. Things became much more expensive a few years ago due to the arrival of our new currency, the euro. The Irish, with much wringing of hands, traded in their old pounds and pence for euro and cent, thinking that they were going to get ripped off in the process. And you know what? They were right.

It seemed like just about every retailer in this country took advantage of the currency confusion to increase prices. In many cases, and depending on the product, prices soared skyward by over twenty percent.

But we weren't the only country to suffer from price increases. Our neighbours in the so-called 'Euro Zone' did too. France, Germany, Italy, Spain...all of their citizens complained about the magical increases in the cost of everything from cheese to candy bars as they swapped local currencies for the new common one.

All that I can say is that we're only going to get one currency change in our lifetime, so retailers won't have the opportunity of again pulling the wool over our eyes. But while prices have grown higher, and though we bitch and moan, is Ireland really so expensive?

Yes, some things really are expensive, as has been outlined above. The cost of housing and almost anything having to do with running a car seems laughably overpriced. Taxation, both direct and indirect, significantly adds to the burden. But other things seem fairly equal to what you might be paying in the United States, Europe, and many other places around the globe. And some aspects of the Irish way of living remain absolute bargains.

Food: when comparing food prices here with those in the United States or the Continent I'm fairly confident that many prices are on just about an even footing. Yes, some things here are more expensive, particularly if they have to be imported. Much of Ireland's fruit and vegetables (everything from apples to oranges to potatoes – that's right, potatoes) are now imported. The small population and shipping costs mean that we pay much more than others do for these items. And frankly, the quality might not be up to scratch.

Too, Irish manufacturers do not offer 'value' packs of products like those that are available Stateside. This means that most consumers here – despite comparatively larger family sizes – pay over the odds for many consumables including baked beans, peanut butter (yes, they finally distribute peanut butter in Ireland), frozen garden peas, and other products.

But to be fair, Ireland does have its deals. Open markets are available in most towns and larger villages. Prices for many food items, including fresh and canned foods, are lower there. Value for money is also available in bakeries. Though the price for a loaf of bread might seem more expensive than elsewhere, the taste and nutrition of the product can't be beat. Like anywhere else, you get what you pay for and you have to shop around. Two-for-one promotional packs of many food items are often available. It might cost a little more here to keep food on the table, but not by much.

Clothing: it's true that if you're looking for designer wear you'll pay through the nose. But if you're looking to simply keep yourself warm – and don't mind purchasing where everyone else does – you'll find Ireland something of a bargain. Major Irish department stores offer just about everything for everybody: kids clothes to adult, underwear to suits, it's on offer.

Local retail shops can also be a source for bargains. That said, boutiques can be rather pricey but are still a great source for the latest in Italian fashion. And men's speciality shops can be the source for great bargains in suits. I buy all of my suits here (not that I have many) and often save substantial sums when compared to the U.S. That said, an Irish friend of mine, recently returned from visits to both Europe and the States, raved about the bargains to be had there for men's clothes when compared to Ireland. So it pays to shop around.

If you're looking for clothes bargains in Ireland, try the local drapers. A 'draper' does not seem to have a U.S. equivalent, though a typical country store back home comes very close. Drapers sell just about anything that can be made of cloth: from curtains to towels to clothing. And it's great fun to sort through mountains of material in search of that special bargain.

However, you might want to hear what my wife and daughters have to say on the matter. Clothing is a way of life for them and they constantly bitch about the comparable prices of buying 'glad rags' in Ireland.

Their counsel is this: when it comes to ladies undergarments, jeans, blouses, towels, and bed linen the U.S. and Continental Europe win hands down on both quality and price. Every time we venture back to the States, the women in my life make a beeline to the closest strip mall in search of new supplies. If you're planning on venturing this way, perhaps visit your local shopping mall to stock up. For instance, I was planning a trip to Tampa recently and decided that, prior to departure, I'd buy myself a new pair of jeans. I priced Wranglers at our local men's shop and discovered that they wanted over fifty euro for a pair – approximately sixty-five dollars. I decided to wait and it's a good thing that I did. Upon arriving back in the U.S. I visited my parent's local Wal-Mart. I bought the same Wrangler jeans for a measly fourteen bucks.

That's quite a savings. Still, I don't think that we're being completely ripped-off here when it comes to clothing. Look around. You'll find good clothing at competitive prices.

Furniture: Ireland is renowned for its furniture. In fact, I live in the furniture capital of the country. As it turns out, Navan has more furniture factories per square mile than any other town in the land. You'll find the fashion in furniture to be quite different than back home not only in basic design but also in the selection of fabrics on offer. If you're into Early American you'd better bring it with you because Ireland doesn't make it. Ireland does, however, now import extensively from Europe. So if you're from the Continent you'll find designs that are quite familiar, but at inflated prices.

Quality, like everywhere else in the world, has declined over the years, but Irish furniture company owners still take pride in their work. Spend a reasonable sum on your furniture and it will last you for years.

Electrical Equipment: as alluded to above, the cost of electrical goods in this country has tumbled in recent years and the selection has increased along with everyone else's. You can buy just about anything you can think of for reasonable prices. It's true that in some cases you might pay over the odds for the most recent technology (DVD players were outrageously expensive here when they first came out but I gather that the same was true Stateside and on the Continent; prices have since tumbled), but competition and the law of survival of the fittest quickly plays to the hands of the consumer.

Everything from TV's to washing machines, stereo systems to freezers can now be had for no more than what you'd pay in the U.S and Europe. But be prepared to be startled at differences in design. Refrigerators, for instance, are much smaller than in the U.S. and rarely come with external ice machines (recently, however, U.S.-sized refrigerators have become available to Irish consumers but at prices much more than in the States). Garbage disposals are almost non-existent (I had to look everywhere for mine and I suspect that we're one of the few homes in the country capable of grinding its leftovers into oblivion).

Washing machines are also smaller than their U.S. equivalent and are invariably front-loaders, and the same can be said of dryers. My wife constantly bugs me to purchase a U.S.-built pair of machines for her weekly washing. It seems that some smart guy in Dublin started importing them, and has also reworked the motor to handle the difference in electrical current. This has only given my wife another excuse to attack me for more cash. But while it is true that the larger size would make her daily chores more efficient, the cost of the U.S. imports are astronomical. Too, they're so big compared to Irish machines that I'd have to rebuild the utility room.

As previously mentioned, Ireland operates on 240 volts so if you're coming from the States be aware that bringing along your electrical equipment is often not a good idea. That said, people in the construction industry often use U.S. manufactured power tools, coupling them to a transformer to make the voltage transition.

Immigrants from Continental Europe have much less to worry about in that their countries already operate on 240 volts. Be aware that the only difference is in the shape of Irish electrical plugs. These conform to U.K. standards so Europeans from other countries are advised to bring along a slew of plug converters or buy new ones here and refit their appliances.

Cars and Car Insurance: anything having to do with the trusty motorised buggy is expensive here. But you can save money in a couple of ways. First, don't buy a new car. A new car purchased in Ireland can cost over thirty to fifty percent of the price of its U.S. or European equivalent. So consider sticking to a good used car. Remember too that because of petrol prices cars are smaller here, compared to the U.S anyway. Forget the benefits of an eight-cylinder engine. Most European cars come with four cylinders. But better technology, including the development of sixteen-valve engines, means that our little buggies can still pack a wallop.

Because of the new prosperity here people have been buying new cars like wildfire, and used car lots are awash with chunks of metal that hopeful salesmen would just as soon be rid of. Many of these vehicles are only one or two years old and in good shape. Make a reasonable offer and you'll soon be on the road.

Second, consider importing your car from the U.S. or Europe. While an American car and many European vehicles are obviously left hand drive – and we drive on the other side of the road over here – it will work just fine. Parts can be a problem, but most everything is available at a modest price from the United Kingdom and they will be delighted to deliver it to you using a 24-hour shipping facility.

You can also purchase a car in the U.K. for thirty percent less (or even less than that) than in Ireland and ship it in. Car prices in the U.K. are much lower due both to stiffer competition in that part of the world (and subsequently a different pricing structure) and because taxes there are, naturally, much less. The Brits love their cars. They'd never let the government away with a significant increase in car taxes like we Irish have.

However, the Irish government will hit you with a tax bill (based on the value of the car) when importing it. Despite that, importing a vehicle can still work out to be a great deal. For instance, a friend of mine decided that following many years of toil he wanted to reward himself by purchasing a previously owned Jaguar. He looked around in local Irish garages. The price for predictably clapped out Jag's with fifty to seventy thousand miles on the clock was in excess of twenty thousand euro.

So instead he resorted to the Internet. After a bit of research he found a garage located in the midlands of England that was selling a pretty nice 1998 Jaguar. It was as clean as a whistle and looked showroom new. With only forty thousand miles on the odometer he suspected that it was still in good condition.

He flew over on a Thursday and brought it back by ferry the following day. The total price including the Irish government's tax levy was a measly thirteen thousand euro. Buying a car outside of Ireland and importing it makes all sorts of economic sense.

Four other items while I'm on the subject of automobiles:

Insurance: automobile insurance premiums in Ireland are scandalous and the insurance companies are under constant scrutiny by government watchdogs for anti-competitive behaviour and price fixing. Teenage boys are the worst hit. I recently heard about a lad who had purchased a good used car. The kid was twenty-one years of age, drove a car sporting a 1.3 litre engine (a small car), and was fairly responsible. He asked for quotes from three companies. The best quote he received was over five thousand euro for one year of insurance. And that was simply for fire and theft.

Needless to say, the kid's new car is still sitting in the drive and the young man thinks that he'll spend the rest of his days riding a bicycle thereby foregoing any opportunity of dating the local girls.

If you're young, and even if you're good looking, be prepared to pay exorbitantly for the privilege of driving here.

Older folk can fare much better. For instance, I'm driving a two-litre SUV and paying just over five hundred euro a year for full coverage. I think that's as competitive a price as I'd get anywhere.

But remember this one piece of advice: no matter what age you are, get a letter from your present insurance company stating that you've been driving for over five years without an accident.

Why, you may ask? It's this simple. Insurance companies here offer what they call a 'No Claims Bonus'. If you have a no claims bonus you will be eligible to receive up to 70 percent off the 'standard rate' of an insurance premium. As an example: over twelve years ago I did something stupid and had an accident. It was my fault and I lost my no claims bonus.

My insurance bill prior to the accident was four hundred Irish pounds. Following the accident it had more than tripled. It took me five years of accident-free driving to prove to the insurance company that I was once again a safe bet. Only then did my premium rates come down.

If you are a safe driver, you have to prove it. Bring that letter from your insurance company or broker along with you when you move here.

NCT Tests: if you own a car that is four years old or older you must prove to the government that it is road worthy. For that reason you must take your car for an NCT test (National Car Test). If you don't take your car to be tested it can be suddenly impounded. But take heart. Your car isn't the only vehicle in Ireland that must be tested. Rather, you and every other Irish person must take your car to a specially authorised garage that will give it the once over.

These tests are, if you pardon me, another way for the government to remove money from our ever-thinning wallets, but that's the law. The cost is only thirty euro or so but once every two years you must bring down the old jalopy for its check-up. The testers put it through its mechanical paces: checking lights, tyre quality, engine fitness, and otherwise making certain that your family auto isn't going to fall apart anytime soon. And if your buggy fails the test you must have the offending item fixed before your car will be declared roadworthy. If you do not have the item(s) repaired within a fixed period of time, and you continue to drive the offending vehicle, your modest buggy can be impounded.

Most cars are so well cared for at this point, and so new, that an NCT test seems to be a waste of time. However, make sure that you comply with this procedure. Otherwise you're breaking the law.

Road Tax: like the U.S., Britain, and Europe, everyone owning a car in Ireland pays an annual tax on his or her auto. This so-called Road, or Motor, Tax is charged based on the size of the car's engine. The bigger the engine the more tax you'll pay.

Unlike most countries in Europe and almost all States in the U.S., however, you'll be in for a shock when you get the bill. Road Tax in Ireland is expensive, with the lowest rate (for a car powered by two squirrels and a rubber band) being over two hundred euro per annum and thereafter climbing into the stratosphere. If you want to impress your friends and neighbours with a Humvee powered by a ten-litre engine you will not only find it uncomfortable to drive on our narrow roads but you'd also better be prepared to pay the tax for such luxury.

Driver's Licences: for the first three months or so of residency (or more if you're lucky and no one finds out) your U.S. licence will work just fine over here. Thereafter, you must get an Irish driver's licence. Like the U.S. you'll have to take both a written and practical examination. I suggest paying a few quid for lessons at a local driver's training school. They know what they're doing, can significantly increase your odds of passing the test, and won't panic when you suddenly go into a fugue-state, think that you're back in Philadelphia, and choose to drive your vehicle on the wrong side of the road.

Driver's examinations are the province of the local county council so contact your nearest for more information when you get into town. Do it soon because an avalanche of new would-be drivers has put incredible pressure on the time that it takes to schedule a test. My daughter recently applied for her test and was told that she couldn't be scheduled in for another eight months.

Driver's licences are still a good deal, however, with a ten-year licence costing only fifty euro or so.

Do note: if you are a North American citizen moving to this country you will not be able to get automobile insurance until you receive your driver's licence. So plan accordingly.

European drivers coming to Ireland from other European Communities will find that their existing EU driver's licences will do just fine in this country.

The Cost of Higher Education

While it is true that Ireland can be expensive (just ask anyone who has managed to survive here) there are many aspects to this country that are incredible bargains. One of the great bargains to be had is the incredible value of education.

If you are a citizen of Ireland and happen to have one or two – or more – children, you'll find the financial planning for their higher education something of a doddle. While the Irish may complain about it, and though the present Minister for Education seems to be doing everything in his power to make it more expensive, Ireland is almost scandalously inexpensive when it comes to the cost of obtaining a diploma.

For instance, two of my children are presently attending college. The cost? Six thousand euro – or about seven thousand, eight hundred dollars – per child per year. And that six thousand includes almost everything: from tuition to rooms to food to books. I pay for it all, of course. If the kids want a beer – which isn't included in that figure – they have to pay for it themselves.

Why so cheap, you may ask? In Ireland, all publicly funded colleges and universities have a set tuition fee of only seven hundred euro per annum or so. In fact, it's not even called tuition. They've branded it as a simple administration fee, which seems fair enough. Of course, you could send your kids to a private school where the costs can increase dramatically but the quality there isn't guaranteed. Better to keep them in public universities and colleges.

What's more, that standard inexpensive fee is applied to every public institute of higher learning: from the great halls of Trinity College right down to the smaller local institutes and regional technical schools.

Seven hundred euro per annum seems to buy a lot, doesn't it?

Having moved here you can of course send your child back to the U.S. or Europe for their education if that's your preference. My daughter wanted to do that. Playing to my pride, she one day asked me if it would be possible for her to attend my old undergraduate Alma Mater. Naturally, I was somewhat pleased with the fact that she wanted to follow in my footsteps so I agreed to look into the matter.

I phoned the Admissions Department.

'Hi,' I said. 'I'm a graduate from ought-six and my daughter is thinking of attending the old homestead.'

'That's wonderful,' the Registrar stated gleefully, undoubtedly thinking of the large sum that he would see for the benefit of winning over another sucker. 'When was she thinking of starting?'

'Next year.'

'Oh, then I'd better start filling in the application form for you. Admissions are just around the corner you know. Name, please?'

'Just a second,' I stated. 'Before we get into that can I ask how much this costs?'

'What?'

'You know. The tuition and what not.'

The line hissed with static, then he cleared his throat. 'Well actually it's a mere…' His voice trailed off into a barely audible whisper.

'Would you repeat that?' I asked.

He said it again and I almost fell out of my chair. One year of tuition and full board was going to set me back over twenty five thousand bucks. Which meant that I was going to spend a hundred grand before she finally graduated from college.

I quietly hung up the telephone.

My daughter has since gone on to a wonderful college in the Midlands of Ireland where she is majoring in business studies. She seems quite happy. And at less than a quarter of what I'd be paying if I'd sent her to the States, I'm happy too.

Similarly expensive fees can be charged in much of mainland Europe. And while the quality of education in the U.K. or on the Continent can be wonderful, I'm completely satisfied with the quality of schooling in Ireland.

Going to college or university here can be a wonderful journey. The quality of education is first rate, and while Irish colleges might not have the breadth of courses on offer compared to many U.S., U.K. or Continental institutions, students can still select from any number of courses: everything from law to medicine, fine arts to marine biology, business and accounting to engineering and math.

For years Ireland has been renowned for the quality of its school system, as well as its graduates. This country's higher education system constantly ranks highly against colleges located in both the U.S. and Europe. For that reason, American companies and their European counterparts have recognised the high quality of students graduating from Irish institutions, viewing this potential workforce as a resource to be tapped. For many years, and because of Ireland's dire economy, newly graduated Irish men and women would have to go abroad to realise their personal ambitions. Now, however, the international economic mountain is coming to Ireland, snapping up these individuals and employing them in industry as accountants, IT personnel, human resource staff, and hundreds of other positions.

Irish colleges and universities represent some of the best value for money in this country. For that reason, if for no other, I have elected to stay here.

But the university system isn't the only aspect of the Irish educational structure that brings a smile to my face. The quality of education in the lower levels of the system is fantastic, too. My kids have all benefited from an educational infrastructure and teachers that are devoted to the basics. Not only are my children now literate and numerate, but I also like to think that their Irish education has prepared them well for their futures, and whatever they want to make of them.

A Survivor's Guide to Living in Ireland

Do I Bring Everything or Do I Leave It All Behind?

When I came here and as already mentioned I was broke. Consequently, I could never have afforded to bring all of our household contents. But in the past few years a number of friends of mine who have considered immigrating have always asked me a standard question: should I bring everything with me when I come or should I leave it behind?

Twenty years ago I would have suggested that they bring everything over, even the kitchen sink. But things have changed and I've reversed my advice.

In my considered opinion only bring with you those personal effects that you absolutely must have and those items that you might need to get you through the first few months. Shipping anything else will be a waste of money.

Again, remember the difference in voltages. So if you're from America leave behind your refrigerator and washer. Your hair dryer and vacuum. Your thirty-six inch television and expensive, custom-built hi-gain radio. Even consider ditching your PC for a new one (unless, of course, it comes with a built in transformer in which case you're all set). Dell Computers has one of the largest manufacturing units in the world on the west coast of this country. Like the U.S., they sell excellent product at inexpensive prices. Instead of bringing your old computer with you consider burning your PC's documents onto a series of CD's or portable hard drive and reinstall it all on a brand new PC when you get here.

Rather than bring everything I suggest that you sell (or store) your furniture and get rid of the lawn mower. The weight to value ratio simply means that it makes little sense to ship it all over when you can purchase similar items here at prices that are not that much different from back home. Too, imports might attract import duties, taxes that should be avoided at all costs.

The only thing that you might consider bringing over is your car (which I've already discussed) and your pet turtle – assuming that you can get it through customs.

Speaking of pets: Ireland is rabies-free which means that the Irish aren't particularly keen on seeing immigrants of the four-footed variety. You'll soon learn that bringing in a pet to the State of Ireland requires your friendly Poodle to spend a minimum of six months in quarantine to ensure that he or she is clear of that most rabid of diseases. Consider carefully whether or not you want your feline or canine best friend to spend such a long period of time in prison prior to release.

But if Ireland is so expensive, why come here at all? Yes, on average Ireland really is more expensive than many places within the United States and Europe. Yes, it can now cost a comparable fortune to run a car and buy a house. But despite these facts thousands and thousands of people immigrate to this country every year.

Why, you may ask, do they do such a thing? For many reasons, of course. But one of the best is quite straightforward: they come because Ireland is so beautiful.

Guideline Seven
Come for the Pleasure of it All

Tampa, Florida   *January 5, 2001*

Dear Son,

It's been almost twenty years now since you bravely started to march to your own drum. After so long, you undoubtedly have learned to cope with living in such a different society. Your mother and I simply hope that you are happy with such a long-term decision.

And though we've been at loggerheads for years, I do know that you've raised some great kids. Our grandchildren have obviously benefited from what is a wonderful country.

Continuing to Love You Despite Everything,

Dad/Grandpa

P.S. It's 90 degrees under sunny skies here as I enjoy my retirement in our brand new home that cost only a few thousand bucks even though it sits on the tenth tee of the golf course. I hope that you are enjoying the rain and expensive housing in your new country. If you should change your mind about living there, and are contemplating a return to what really is your rightful home, do give us a call. We miss you…

I was talking to the U.S. Embassy the other day and was informed by them that – get this – over sixty thousand citizens of the United States now call Ireland home. That's right. *Sixty thousand.* Add to that the thousands of immigrants coming to these shores from countries in the European Union as well as Canada, Australia, Nigeria, the Balkan states, and farther a-field, and you quickly realise the Ireland must have something very special to offer.

Certainly, all of these people couldn't be wrong. So what's so wonderful about Ireland?

A Survivor's Guide to Living in Ireland

My Dad's take on the country is probably a good indication. Though he was positively horrified that I had moved here with his grandchildren, placing a mere ocean between us, and though he had stopped talking to me because of this, I eventually won him around.

I did it cleverly enough, I think. In 1984 I invited him to spend some time here with us. It took some doing (including the promise of never again asking him for money) but we eventually convinced both of my parents to come out for a visit. Dad, with much grumbling, bought the tickets and they came over.

I picked up my parents from the airport on a miserable summer's morning. As usual, it was raining. It was cold. The wind was blowing. Both of my parents were not impressed. 'What a lovely country!' my mother lied as she shivered beneath her thick overcoat. 'Bah!' my father said, obviously annoyed by the trouble of crossing thousands of miles and numerous time zones in an economy seat much too small for comfort.

Dad was in a bad mood. If he had his way, he would be spending a couple of weeks on a Hawaiian beach somewhere. But because I had begged him for months to at least try it here, he had instead agreed to bask in the cool, temperate, but rainy climate of Ireland, if only for a few days.

I drove the car up and saw him standing at the airport's Arrival's curb, his summer coat turned up against the miserable weather, his facial expression fixed in that particular way that suggested he was not having a good time.

I stopped the car and grabbed their bags.

'When does the sun shine?' he asked grumpily.

'It always rains here,' I explained. 'It rains even when it's supposed to be summer. It rains so much that often we don't recognise the sun when it eventually chooses to shine on us. We stand staring up at it, saying: "Look, Maggie! What's that yellow orb in the sky?" But you'll like it despite that fact. Honest. Just try to be open-minded.'

'Open minded my ass,' he mumbled as he squeezed himself into my tiny Ford Fiesta, a car a good five sizes too small for him. He became resigned to two weeks of misery.

But my wife and I had already talked about the visit and were determined to win both of them over. Rather than stay in Navan and increase Dad's displeasure by imprisoning him in the postage stamp-sized council house with no central heating, we hit on the incredibly wonderful idea of taking him to West Cork.

West Cork, which is a region in the west of County Cork as fate would have it, is a place unto its own. I had learned quickly about the quirkiness of that region of the country during my first job. In search of potential sales for my weighbridge company, and having decided to visit some of the more hidden places of Ireland, I had managed to become incredibly lost.

In those early days, and without the benefit of a satellite navigation system, and even though I owned a good map, I could find myself lost almost anywhere in the country on even the driest, clearest of days. This was due, perhaps, to two reasons: first, and because of history, Ireland has literally thousands of miles of roadways snaking between her shores. The second reason is due to a decided lack of adequate road signage. The Irish seem to hate signs, particularly those that would effectively help a visitor to get from A to B. While I've never been able to prove it I suspect that the Irish rather enjoy it when foreigners get lost in their land, driving from one end of the country to the other, always on the lookout for some sort of landmark, always hoping that they will eventually get to where they want to go. Perhaps this propensity goes back to the British occupation, as a sort of defensive measure. After all, if the enemy could go astray within the confusing labyrinth of Ireland's unmarked road system, there was a good chance that they would starve to death before finding any source of succour. And that would be one less John Bull to worry about.

Even to this day Ireland's smaller roads can lack an adequate navigation system. And in that many of the smaller back roads are lined by high hedges that prevent a driver from gaining a reasonable view of the surrounding countryside (often precluding the discovery of landmarks that might instantly help you to locate yourself), and because these road can look so very similar to each other, and due to the fact that the sun is often obscured by an overhang of grey cotton clouds thereby giving the driver no clue as to whether he or she is heading north, south, east or west, you could well think that you were driving toward Cork when in fact you are actually heading back to Dublin.

A Survivor's Guide to Living in Ireland

The fact that many roads are not signed – or are signed poorly or obscurely – make journeys interesting in that a person might never quite be certain where they really are. For instance, I might be driving down a country road trying to get to Ballydehob. Map in hand, I'll come to a crossroads and…no road signs. I'll strain my neck hoping to take note of signage buried behind a tree or stuck on the wrong side of a barn. Not a chance. With no signage I'll have no idea whether to turn right, left, go straight ahead, or perhaps turn around and go back in the direction from which I came. The decided lack of signage can promote heart palpitations, backache, dizziness, and general frustration. But one thing is for certain: a trip is always an adventure.

Things have improved a bit over the years, but frankly it's not that much better. Trying to give directions to a person unfamiliar with the country is akin to sending people on a journey to the dark side of the Moon. With no reference points to help them, you can only point them down a road and hope for the best.

Don't expect a map to help, either. Once lost on the internal roads of Ireland it is quite possible that you might never be found again. When travelling, it's best to pack a survival kit suitable for excursions into the interiors of Antarctica as a safeguard against possible starvation and hypothermia.

It's a wonder that more foreign visitors haven't disappeared into the Irish road system without a trace.

Ireland is connected by a road network composed of thousands and thousands of miles of blacktop, potholed though they might be. Most of these roads don't seem to go anywhere and I've often wondered why they were built in the first place. With the dawn of the Celtic Tiger the National Roads Authority, the government agency responsible for road infrastructure development, has embarked on a courageous campaign to improve the state of Irish roads. But the task that they face is monumental. The entire population of this country expects that in a few short years the NRA will fix a problem that took generations to create. While they have managed to make great progress over the past five years – Ireland now has a few miles of Motorway, but I assure you it will never rival the Highway systems of either America, Germany or England – they still have a great deal of work left to do.

Despite millions and millions of euro poured into road development and maintenance, we in Ireland continue to enjoy some of the worst roads in Europe. We've come to joke about the fact that the potholes in Ireland can often swallow entire cars, and the subsequent wear and tear on suspension systems, gear boxes, tyres, and the people who drive them has a great deal to do with the fact that a new car in this country rarely gets more than ten years of usable life.

It's no wonder that the Irish government instituted the NCT Test.

But back to my first trip to West Cork. On that particular day I had turned off onto a back road and within a very few minutes felt my stomach heave slightly as I experienced the faint possibility that I was lost. I turned down another road, then another, trying to find my way back to the main thoroughfare, but to no avail. Finally, I pulled the car over – an ancient Ford Cortina Estate that had been assigned to me by my new employer – and studied my trusty map. Not that it was going to help. Because of the lack of signage I had no idea what road I might now be parked on, which meant that I had not the faintest possibility of determining even an approximate location of where I was. And if I had no idea where I was, I hadn't the foggiest notion of how I might get to where I hoped to go.

I had been journeying to a small farm holding owned by a certain Mr Hanratty who would undoubtedly be displeased with my inept attempt to sell him an all-singing, all-dancing forty-foot long weighbridge and who would undoubtedly throw me off of his land with much screaming and hollering. However, motivated as I was by impending destitution and the cries of a starving family, I had decided to throw caution to the wind and try to win the sale anyway.

But having become lost, it was now highly possible that Mr Hanratty would not have to put up with my poor sales strategy, and having become lost on the narrow back roads of West Cork I began to wonder if I would ever be found and instead die of starvation.

I finally got out of the car and stood in the middle of the road, shivering slightly in the misting rain, and looked down the spaghetti-thin line of tarmac as it disappeared over the far horizon.

No car, no person, not a living thing could be seen. I looked in the other direction. Nothing. I was not only lost, but as happenstance would have it, I had become lost in an area seemingly devoid of any breathing human from whom I might possibly get directions.

Prayer crossed my mind.

And then as fate would have it I saw in the distance a small dot make its way over the winding roadway. The dot slowly grew until I beheld a man on a bicycle. I flagged him down thinking that I had found salvation.

As I keep saying, things have changed in Ireland since those early days of my immigration. But the sight that I beheld back then was something straight out of an Irish tourist guidebook or an old illustration about this country's colourful past.

He was an older man, possibly in his mid-seventies. His face was lined and creased and held a few day's growth of stubble on his cherry cheeks but despite his age he pumped at the rickety two-wheeler of his as if his life depended on it. His black torn trousers were tied up with a length of rope possibly used for hangings back in the days of the Old IRA. In his teeth he gripped the stump of a pipe and on his head he had perched a fading pork-pie cap that had obviously seen too many days of revelry. He rode an ancient Raleigh bike that had possibly been used during the Emergency, what the Irish government had in its wisdom chosen to call those terrible days of the Second World War.

What approached me was a vision out of the mid-nineteenth century and upon seeing the distressed stranger who was waving like a madman at the side of the road, the ghostly vision coasted to a stop in front of me and dismounted.

He doffed his cap, wiped his brow, then like the vast majority of the people of Ireland, he greeted me warmly as if he viewed it as his solemn duty to help a stranger in distress.

I was saved. I would find my destination in no time, convince Mr Hanratty of the significant benefits of weighbridges, close the deal, and be back to my wife with the good news of not only a substantial bonus but the possibility of an immediate raise. And then the old man opened his mouth and I knew that I was in trouble.

A Survivor's Guide to Living in Ireland

You see, the people in the west of Cork speak in English like everyone else in Ireland. However, they speak it in such a way as to be absolutely unintelligible to almost anyone living outside of their area. It seems that you have to be born and raised there if you're going to gain an ear for their impossible albeit wonderful local accent.

'Ah!' he croaked. 'And a whashimish do ye hassat in de beer rood?'

I nodded, possibly looking like a lunatic, as I attempted to understand him. 'It is a fine day, isn't it?' I said, thinking that like many here he had made his opening shot at conversation with his views on the weather. 'I'm afraid I'm lost. Could you help me?'

'Nossa problem, ye weefellayou weer. Assa bein goin afer, ahye?'

I needed an interpreter but none was to be found on that rainy summer day. I raised my voice, in that moronic manner that people have when talking to someone who speaks in foreign tongues, as if more vocal volume might help my plight. 'I'm looking for the Hanratty's? Do you know them? I think they live around here somewhere? It's a large farm?'

I had involuntarily sunk into the verbal repartee of treating the old man like an idiot savant. The old man, however, didn't seem to mind at all.

After much to-ing and fro-ing, and fumbling attempts at extracting the necessary information from language that I could understand only with great difficulty, here are the directions that I finally received:

'Well, lad. If it's the Hanratty's that you're looking for you've taken the wrong road.'

He sniffed, possibly thinking that I should have stayed in bed that morning or should have at least hired a guide to lead me through the savage back-lands of the Old Country. 'What you need to do is turn around and go back to Murphy's house at the bridge. Do you know where that is? Not the old man Murphy's, now, but his Young 'Un.

'Then you turn and go down to where the pub used to be before it was burned to the ground in the fire. You'll know it because of the new growth of fabulous vegetation that's hidden the foundation. Turn left there, travel along the road for a mile or two –

or maybe a few more – and you'll find the Hanratty place on the right, behind the hill that overlooks the river that you can't quite see from the road.'

'Thank you, sir,' I replied, knowing that I had come no further in finding my way to the Hanratty's.

'And toyerself, and Godbegoodtoyou, so loofarna, now. Slàn!'

With that he climbed back on his bike and tranquilly peddled off into the distance, certain to share his conversation about the idiot Yank over his next pint with friends and family.

I chose to abandon the quest for the Hanratty's and eventually found my way back to Cork City where I instantly rang my wife, who as it turned out had become nervous at my failure to ring her on our brand new telephone, and told her that she could stand-down the search and rescue operation and that I had survived the back roads of Ireland.

The only person who never forgave me for getting lost was my boss who became annoyed that I had also lost the sale.

With any luck, you will be able to survive the back roads of Ireland too. Of course, you could simply hide in the bigger cities, there to be almost certain that you will never find yourself lost, but the adventures of discovering the secrets of back-of-beyonds Ireland will certainly prove too much for you to resist.

The Captivation of Ireland

When we had decided to plan my parent's trip, we instantly determined to take them to West Cork simply because it is so beautiful there. It had been over a year since my misdirected adventure and the old man's directions, and with twelve months under my belt I had decided that I could successfully navigate the roads of Ireland to just about anywhere that they might lead me.

My mother was game for anything and had no objections to the adventure. My father was more doubtful but would do anything to get out of the teensy council house. Hence, we piled most of our luggage into our tiny Ford Fiesta car and the rest into the tiny Fiat car that my father had rented and determined to start our journey.

For what seemed like days my parents experienced the jolting nightmare of Ireland's potholes as we travelled through Dublin and thence to Cork City. We turned west there, and began the three-hour trip to the coastline.

When we arrived at our destination my father looked like he was ready to have a heart attack. Either that or kill me. He was incensed at the poor roadways, stressed by the lack of courtesy that Irish drivers then (and now) showed each other, and otherwise believed that he was lucky to be alive.

'I'm getting us the hell out of here before we all get killed!'

I had thought that our plans to win him over had completely backfired.

And then he walked into the cottage.

As it turned out we had planned our trip well. My wife and I, at what then had been a fairly considerable expense, had rented a holiday cottage in Skull, a tiny village located on the south-western edge of the County of Cork. We had not had the opportunity of seeing for ourselves what the cottage – or its local environs – had on offer. We could only believe what we had seen in the tourist brochure.

Fortunately for me, what the brochure had said in print turned out to be true in reality. And it saved the fracturing relationship with my father.

The cottage was, in fact, a brand new two-storey affair with all of the mod-cons at our fingertips. It held a large kitchen, a fully furnished and very comfortable living room, a wonderfully situated coal-burning fireplace, three large and airy bedrooms complete with adjoining bathrooms, and it had central heating.

My father was impressed.

He was even more impressed when he saw the view. It was spectacular. The cottage was situated above a bay with an absolutely incredible panorama of a sun-streaked ocean, followed in the evening by positively picturesque scenes as the sun set. He watched the view while my good wife and I made dinner: Irish bacon, fresh cabbage, spring potatoes, and an apple tart that was like heaven on earth.

My father was even more impressed.

With his belly full, we decided to take a little turn around the small village. 'How about a pint of Guinness at the local pub?' I suggested innocently.

'What's a Guinness?' Dad asked. He lived a sheltered life. In short order, we made our way down to the local establishment.

It will take another book to adequately describe the warmth of welcome that the Irish have for the thousands of visitors that travel through their country every year. The Irish are unlike any other populace that I've ever had the good fortune to know. Except for dark, dismal places that one occasionally finds here and within which the local people treat a stranger like some sort of East Asian disease, the vast majority of Irish people greet even the strangest of strangers like some long lost relative.

My father, living as he has for most of his life in the vast, faceless spaces of American suburbia, was initially quite suspicious. 'Who are they and what do they want?' he asked sceptically upon receiving a warm welcome from Joe the Publican who plied his wares from behind the solid mahogany bar. 'If he thinks he's going to take me for a fool, I'll call the Marines on him and give him a beating that he'll never forget.'

'He's Irish, Dad. Give him a break.'

Joe plopped a Pint of the Best down in front of my father. Dad viewed the dark brew even more sceptically. Not knowing any better, he picked it up immediately and prepared to quaff the drink like an insipid lager.

'For God's sake, man, let it settle!' Joe squealed. Dad, of course, thought that this was the height of rudeness. But when I told Joe that my father was an American tourist and didn't know any better, and then told Dad the secrets of a correct pint of Guinness, both looked at each other with a new respect and decided to give the other the benefit of the doubt.

If you haven't experienced a pint of Guinness for yourself you're in for a treat. Guinness is unlike any other beer in the world. There is a fine art to both the pouring and the drinking of a pint, and if you don't obey the rules be prepared to be treated with both scorn and derision by the rest of the drinking population.

What will first strike you is the fact that a barkeep will not simply pour a pint to the top of the glass. Rather, he'll pour two-thirds of a pint and put it to the side. Don't think that you're being short-changed, however, because that good publican is only giving his art time to settle.

Though you might be parched and salivating to beat the band you will have to contain your excitement and wait while a marvellous miracle takes place. Tiny bubbles work their way to the top of the pitch-black body of the drink forming a velvety surface that looks like golden snow. This vision of forming excellence is enough to drive a devout Guinness drinker mad.

When the barkeep believes that enough time has passed, only then will he fill the glass to the top. But even then the drinker isn't yet done waiting. He or she must keep their anticipation at bay as the drink again settles. And then, only then, may he or she embark on their journey of liquid self-discovery.

My father, a bona fide Budweiser drinker, kept looking at his watch, the second hand marching by ever more slowly, as the Publican's beady stare prevented him from taking pint in hand and downing the drink. Finally, when the glass had settled to a perfectly black body topped by a "Bishop's Collar,' what every bone fide Irish person entitles that good inch of rich, golden, velvety snow, only then did the Publican nod his approval. And my father drank.

His eyes went wide. His face glazed. His body settled into a position of absolute contentment. 'What is this stuff?' he asked me in amazement.

'It's a pint of Guinness,' I replied.

'I think I'll have another.' And he did.

If you've never had a pint of Guinness, or have only had the opportunity of drinking Guinness in bottles or in lands outside of Ireland, you've probably never had a real pint. True Guinness is poured, not bottled. It is brewed in St James Gate in Dublin and nowhere else. No other drink is quite the same.

My father drank quite a few pints that night. Each pint made him more relaxed, so much so that by the end of the night he was talking like a local to his fellow drinkers. A night out in an Irish pub, with a good pint in hand and willing Irish fellows nearby anxious to share a good joke, start a sing-song, or simply discuss the events of the day, are an unforgettable experience here. If you are lucky enough to enjoy the warm friendliness of an Irish country pub, it will be a golden memory that you will always remember.

It is an even more astonishing experience if you live here. Live here and your pub can quickly become an extension of your living room. You'll get to know the locals as well as – and sometimes better than – your family. Is it any wonder that wives spend so much of their lives walking from pub to pub in vain searches for long lost husbands?

When the clock approached eleven and Joe – from his station behind the bar – sounded the last call we half carried my father into the night. It was high summer and in these northern climes a magical twilight streaks the sky's dome with an ethereal soft light. When the sun finally does shine, the summers of Ireland are something golden, as if Old Sol is reluctant to leave the open hospitality of this famed land. Honestly, on a clear evening with twilight flickering in the western skies long after you would expect it to, it is as if one could reach up and touch the face of God Almighty Himself.

My father looked up in awe.

'Isn't this a wonderful part of the world?' he said almost reverently. Awkwardly, he patted me on the back. 'Maybe you were half-right in moving here.'

I wasn't half-right. I was completely right. Moving to Ireland was one of the best decisions that I have ever made in my life.

Guideline Eight
Deconstructing Your Nationalisms

Recently overheard in a local Irish hotel:

'I wish they'd bloody well shut their mouths and realise that we don't give a good damn about how much they have in their bank account.'

Anonymous Irish woman whispering to a friend about a conversation that she had with an American tourist

---

I was walking along a beach in County Louth, thirty-five miles or so north of Dublin, when an older fellow, his checked trousers and pale blue jacket announcing to the world that he was an American tourist, walked up to me and started chatting. Having detected my obvious Yankee twang, he began as so many American tourists always do when discovering that I live here and have done so for some time.

Him: 'You're an American. You're on vacation, I take it?'

Me: 'No sir. I live here.'

Him (incredulously): 'You're kidding? How did you manage to do that?'

Me: 'Well, you know, I climbed on an airplane and came over.'

Him: 'How long have you been here?'

Me: 'Just over twenty-three years now.'

He eyed me suspiciously, as if I had just declared my allegiance to the Communist Party or some such thing. Then he took out a large handkerchief, blew his nose, and sniffed loudly.

Him: (sceptically): 'Seems a little unnatural, an American living abroad. (Blustering). You know I live in Levittown. That's in New York, on Long Island.'

Me: 'Yes, sir. I know.'

Him (his voice growing louder): 'I fought in Korea and got married and had three kids and worked my ass off and saved a fortune and I have over half a million bucks in my 401K and my house is paid off and I love my country and George W is a great guy and if any of these cocky Irish people even thinks to criticise the American military's right to enter the Gulf and chase down Saddam, that no good son of a bitch, I'm gonna haul off and slug them right in the nose.'

I suspect that I looked somewhat shocked at this sudden series of personal revelations but the retired soldier never blinked an eye. Instead he stuck out a hand and assumed the role of American Mr Nice Guy, his transition as smooth and as practiced as my Aunt Wilda's homemade split pea soup. 'Well, I'd better get back. The tourist bus is leaving in five minutes. You have a nice day.'

As he marched back along the beach all I could do was sigh.

Americans are renowned throughout the world for their honesty, loyalty, energy, determination, forthrightness, but also – dare I say it – their ability to be a pain in the ass. I'm not saying that every American wears their heart, political persuasion, and total financial net worth on their sleeve the way this guy did but I'll tell you one thing: sometimes my fellow countrymen and women can be downright embarrassing. Usually this is due to one particularly annoying trait: many of my country people don't know when to keep their mouths shut.

I'm generalising when I say it, and of course not every American behaves this way, but I've found that many Red, White and Blue tourists work hard to give the American-bashers plenty of ammunition that allows them to beat the hell out of American values.

In my experience, there are enough Americans on vacation who make it their business to blow off unwanted and inhospitable steam and otherwise seem determined to give the world a bad impression of America that I can begin to understand why Americans abroad have developed the image of bullies among those nations whom they choose to visit.

Worse, these folks will also explain in detail what they don't like about the place that they're visiting and compare that country's downfalls in detail with the privileged lives that they enjoy back Stateside. For instance, I might be enjoying a cup of coffee in a local hostelry, Jury's Inn in Dublin, for example. A tourist bus will pull up and what seems like the entire population of Lowell, Massachusetts will pour off the transport and make their way up to the bar (not that I have anything against Lowell, mind you. Many of my relatives still live in Lowell and I rather like the area).

Anyway, and upon seeing the assorted tourists trouncing like an out of control rugby ruck in my direction, I'll instantly cringe because I'll know what's coming. Anxious not to be associated with them, I'll sidle down toward the other end of the bar, watching in embarrassed silence as the Irish hotel employees, knowing that they are under threat of certain attack, work hard to keep these people satisfied.

First of all, the Americans will be loud. I don't mean just a little noisy. I mean *loud*. Their booming voices can often seem to pack enough decibels to break crockery on the far side of the bar. What is it about many Americans that they think they have to be heard on the other side of the Atlantic even when making a simple observation? Their entrance announced at top volume, I'll put my head in my hands and wait for the pantomime show to start. Often, the pageant will pan out something like this:

An American woman, her thick gold jewellery and magnificent Rolex watch announcing to the world that she is Jane Millionaire, might order a scone. As her tiny treasure is quickly delivered to her, she might say, 'I wanted the scone with margarine, if that's all right with you' to the overworked barkeep as he makes his initial foray into the fray.

'That's fine, madam,' he will state, making a deft recovery. 'That will be an additional fifteen cent.'

'What?' she might reply, as horrified as if she had been asked to pay for the construction of the Panama Canal. 'Fifteen cent? But in America, we don't have to pay any extra for our margarine.'

'I'm sorry, madam,' the barkeep will say, already knowing what's coming. 'But that's the policy at the hotel.'

'Frank? Frank! Come over here.' Frank, her six-foot four-inch ex-linebacker but now retired husband will make his way through the crowd like an incoming battleship.

'What's wrong, honey?' he'll state, instantly assuming that the poor creature whining at his elbow has somehow been assaulted and could very well be dying of knife wounds or worse. 'Is something wrong?'

'Frank, this guy wants me to pay fifteen cent for this tiny little pack of margarine. That's ridiculous. Can't you do something about it?'

Frank, towering above everyone like a living Mount McKinley, will bend down and look the poor barkeep right in the eye and start talking: 'Do you know how much we've spent in your country? Do you realise that without the United States Ireland would be nothing? Aren't you aware that if it weren't for America the world would be a much worse place to live? Don't you know how many Irish, those poor Mick's, have come to our country and made a fortune out of us? And now you want to charge my wife fifteen cent for the privilege of buying a puny packet of margarine? Are you out of your mind?'

At the other end of the bar I bury my head further into a newspaper, doing my best to look like one of the natives, something that I'm now pretty adept at.

The barkeep will clear his throat, realise that he's dealing with a maniac, and do his best to make light of things. 'Now, sir, we do really appreciate the fact that you've found fit to grace this country with your presence. And we have long acknowledged that America is the land of liberty and we are forever beholding to you and yours. But I am only a simple employee and the policy of the hotel is not up to me. You wouldn't want me to lose my job, now, would you sir?'

And with that, the barkeep has managed to turn the tables. The American, now believing that he has the power to make this poor guy's life a misery of future unemployment, will gloriously surrender in a show of Yankee goodwill. He'll reach deep into his pocket and put down not only the requested fifteen-cent, but often an entire twenty-cent coin to boot.

'Ah, shucks. We didn't mean to make any trouble. You just keep the change. Come on, Janie,' he'll say to his now teary-eyed wife, 'let's get out of here.' Having made an emotional mountain out of a packet of margarine, the guy will steer his wife toward the exit, and the poor Irish barkeep's impression that all Americans are crazy will only have been reinforced.

As I say, those Americans of an insensitive nature can be horrible.

A Survivor's Guide to Living in Ireland

It seems that many of my American co-patriots will bitch and moan about almost anything: they'll take exception to the weather (I'll let you in on a secret: it rains quite a bit in Ireland and don't expect otherwise. That's why the grass is always green); they'll complain about the prices (Ireland is expensive and just because you're bringing your hard-earned currency to the country doesn't mean that you're automatically entitled to a discount); they'll laugh at the road network (though it's improving, Ireland still has thousands of miles of potholed roads to make right, and it's going to take a little time to fill in the gaps).

Americans, of course, are not the only nationality to make their opinions about Ireland known to everyone. I've encountered French, German, English, Spanish, and many other nationalities that seem to get some sort of bizarre thrill out of putting down this country, albeit in a manner that is peculiar to their own culture. It seems that citizens visiting – or moving – here from larger, more developed countries can take a while to get used to the place. In the meantime, they risk not only embarrassing themselves but also annoying the locals by comparing Ireland to their homeland.

People from much of North American, Europe, Australia, and similar nations are used to convenience: major stores on every street corner, prices that seem reasonable, transport systems that (usually) work, roads that are paved to be smoother than a baby's bum. And when the Irish reality ends up contrasting so vividly with visitors' mystical impressions of this land – well, it's bound to cause a little resentment. Many people will vent that resentment almost instantly. While they are entitled to do so the manner in which those views are expressed often raise the hackles among the locals.

But I'll let you in on a little secret: most Irish people really don't give a damn about immigrants' and visitors' opinions of their country. And if you're thinking of living here, and unless you want to be treated with scepticism and derision, I'm suggesting that you tone down your act.

As a rule, the Irish are a forgiving lot. They are a peaceful, pleasant, usually welcoming people. But give them enough grief and though they'll take their time about it, they'll get their own back and in some very surprising ways. For instance, a Canadian who had been assigned to live here by his company spent his entire two years doing nothing but bitch about the place: how the food stunk, the fact that the prices were so outrageous, the state of the roads, and on and on and on. His Irish colleagues and neighbours smiled at him, saying nothing for the longest time, instead only doing their best to help him cope with the situation.

Then, toward the end of his stay and with his bitching growing in ever-increasing volumes, one of his neighbours walked up with an old suitcase and suggested to the visitor that he pack his bags, shut his mouth, and kindly leave at the first opportunity.

The Canadian put in for a transfer and was gone within weeks.

If you move here, and while it may seem obvious, you are immigrating into a foreign country. Things are *different* in Ireland. Many of the roads are not up to most U.S. or European standards. The food is different, as is the health system, the education system, business methods, the way that people interact, and the manner in which we all queue for a bus.

It's a different country: a different culture. And if you take some time to quietly listen to it and absorb it, you'll soon learn to appreciate it.

When I first came here in 1982 life in Ireland was tough. I was a spoiled, twenty-something middle-classed American, used to the conveniences and finer things in life that I thought could be found only in the States. Rather than getting over it and accepting what was to be experienced in this delightful country, I began to develop a many-layered coat of resentment. I took peevish pleasure in pointing out to my Irish friends and neighbours what Ireland lacked: at that time, in 1982, Ireland lacked so many things. It was an easy target for criticism.

My Irish neighbours could only shake their heads and hope that the spoiled American would go away.

Over the years I began to appreciate the fact that Ireland had something special to offer, something that I had not permitted myself to see in the first ten years of my residency here. Because of my inability to look over my personal horizons, I made life pretty miserable for myself and almost everyone else around me.

For instance, living in Navan, County Meath as I did and still do, the River Boyne – one of Ireland's most pleasant waterways – was right at my doorstep. Though I took many walks along its peaceful banks my mind was full of what I was missing back in the

United States. The waters sang to me in a magical voice but I never heard it: all I thought about was Italian food, inexpensive telephone systems that worked, and indoor plumbing that held a lifetime supply of hot water. And I'd work myself into a lather, bitching and moaning about how much better life was on the opposite side of the Atlantic.

The Irish, God bless them, only nodded in seeming sympathy. I suspect that they knew that I'd either get over my difficulties in accepting things the way they were – or I'd leave and they'd have one less complaining American to listen to. Not that they would have minded.

If you're reading this book, you are possibly a braver and more resolute person than I was when I moved to this country. You are probably prepared to look over a far horizon toward a new dream and a new life, knowing in your heart that things will be different. Unfortunately, when I came here, my mind was not prepared to accept the reality of something so completely foreign to the land of my birth.

As a potential immigrant, what therefore do you need to do to be happy in your new life among the Irish? One of the first things that you'll need to do is to deconstruct some of your Nationalisms. Whether you are German, Italian or French; American, Canadian or Australian; Polish, Russian or Lithuanian; Nigerian, Tanzanian, or Kenyan, you will have to leave behind many of the personal perceptions that you have been brought up with in order to finally embrace the Ireland of today.

Here are some tips from a guy who almost destroyed himself and everyone else around him during his early life as an immigrant:

Listen rather than talk. You might learn something.

When I first came to Ireland, and like many of my fellow Americans, I took particular pleasure of informing everyone of my absurd belief that I had been specially blessed because I had been born and bred in the United States. And I took almost perverse pleasure in running down Ireland and comparing it to the always-golden country of my birth.

I'm not sure why many Americans take this view. It's a cultural thing, I'm sure. Perhaps it's due to the fact that we say the

Pledge of Allegiance at school every morning. My opinion on the matter is this: from an early age most Americans are taught that our way of life is sacred. After all, it's what the entire population of the rest of the world should aspire to, isn't it? For what other reason would America be a land of continuing immigration? Mexicans aren't risking life and limb by illegally swimming across the Rio Grande River for nothing, are they? America seems to many Americans to be the later day Rome, something that anyone in their right mind aspires to, no matter if they have been born in China, Ireland, France, or Botswana.

Of course, this cultural parochialism isn't limited to Americans. Many British love being British and some refuse to acknowledge that the old Empire is a thing of the past. Quite a few French that I've met believe that the sun rises and sets on their country. And any number of Australians wouldn't trade their huge nation for anywhere else in the world. While cultural patriotism is understandable it can result in problems in that a limited view of the world isn't practical for those of us who, for whatever reason, end up living in another country.

And if you happen to be the type who enjoys vocalising your cultural preferences at the top of your lungs, you'll find getting along in Ireland somewhat more difficult.

Therefore, the simple practice of listening, rather than trumpeting on and on about the privileges that might be found in your particular nation, can make life much easier for everyone, particularly the new immigrant. Listen and you'll soon discover the magic of this country for yourself: the warmth of her people and their love of life; the importance that they attach to family and friends; their willingness to lend a helping hand to those in need.

But insist on blathering on and on like an eejit and you'll soon find that your mind will be closed to the beauty of the country and its people. Keep talking and criticising and all you'll do is piss off the locals. After all, you're a visitor to a new country, aren't you? For that reason, you might let people know that you appreciate the privilege of living here.

Forget your net worth. No one else is going to give a fig about it.

America is the richest nation in the world. Unfortunately, you would be surprised at just how many Americans desire to let the world know that they are significant stakeholders in that wealth. Of course, I've found that this characteristic isn't limited to Americans. I've run into people from many other nations who truly believe that the worth of their persona is intimately tied to how much money they have in the bank.

Honestly, you'd be entirely too surprised – and perhaps ashamed – to know how many times I have been told by an erstwhile visitor to Ireland of the significant funds that they have in their bank accounts, trusts, common stocks, and underneath their mattresses.

It's positively sickening. And often humiliating. For instance, only the other day and while on a quick trip to Cork City, my wife and I had what turned out to be the uncertain opportunity of dining in a well-known restaurant. That night the place was packed. The waitress, a lovely local lass, asked us if we would be willing to share a table with some American tourists. We agreed.

And so we had the pleasure of meeting Jack and Jane (not their real names). They were from New Mexico. They owned a small business. That previous year, Jack's tidy company had generated a net income of over half a million dollars. Between courses Jack also let me know his exact net worth, which happened to be just over four million dollars.

I had trouble eating my soup.

'Yep,' he wore on. 'We've done really well. We work hard. My home is already valued in excess of seven hundred thousand dollars and it's bound to go up. Pass the butter.'

Following this series of revelations, and having known this fellow for exactly fifty-four minutes, Jack proceeded to have a quiet word with our waitress. Unbeknownst to me, and despite my protests when I eventually discovered his intentions, he had arranged to pick up the tab for our dinner. He also left a substantial tip. I suspected that he thought that living as I did in Ireland, I could not possibly afford to buy my wife and I a meal, much less pay for a gratuity. I found his attitude, though certainly well intentioned, absolutely infuriating.

I'm not sure what drives these people to let me know the exact total of their personal fortune. They're not giving any of it to *me*, that's for sure, so why they insist on letting me know of every dollar, Pound Sterling and euro that they've tucked away is beyond me.

The Irish reaction to this declaration of wealth is pretty obvious: they laugh at it. In Ireland, wealth and success – even in the afterglow of the Celtic Tiger economy – is not to be flaunted. Though many young Irish now enjoy the luxuries of driving new BMW's and living in absurdly expensive homes, Irish culture downplays the accumulation and display of wealth.

I suspect that the reasons for this are twofold: first, and for hundreds of years, Ireland has been a land of near poverty. People made do with what they had. Such a culture valued kin and friendship much more than it did money in the bank. The reason for this devaluation of money was simple: though some might dream of wealth, the possibility of creating wealth – except for the few landowners, business people, or English Crown-appointed officials who already possessed wealth – was impossible. Knowing that the possibility of creating a financial mountain was beyond them, most Irish developed aspirations that were obtainable: ownership of a small house and a few acres of land, perhaps; food on the table; close friends; clothes that stood up to the Irish winter. Financial wealth, though interesting, could not be obtained and even considering it was akin to fantasy – much like a brightly glittering coin lying on the bottom of the ocean floor.

The second reason for this downplay of wealth was the Catholic Church. The Church promised a life of happiness in the hereafter and cash just didn't enter into that equation. Money, though a necessary evil, was unimportant. A life of goodness and faith, an existence that sought to love thy neighbour as thyself, was more important than any pot of gold no matter how large.

In many ways, the creation of wealth was viewed as a sin. And if you were lucky enough to have acquired it the only way to Heaven was to give it all away. That philosophy is, in many ways, still fostered in the Irish psyche: many wealthy Irish seem positively guilty about the good fortune that they might enjoy. And though they would rather be richer than poorer, they choose not to display that wealth for fear that their neighbours would begrudge them that good fortune. Often, wealth in Ireland is hidden behind closed doors.

Even the poorest of the Irish do what they can to help others. Ireland's population gives more per capita to the world's impoverished and disenfranchised than any other country in the world. For instance, Ireland's reaction to the recent Indonesian Tsunami was breathtaking in its beneficence. Young, old, rich, poor – it made no difference – the Irish gave and gave and gave. By giving, the Irish not only illustrate the goodness of their hearts, but also I think, the guilt that they continue to suffer regarding money and the deep belief – often never vocalised but always present – that the doorway to Heaven will be opened through simple generosity.

In Ireland the best advice is this: Don't flaunt your wealth unless you desire a constant stream of suspicion and un-stated ridicule. While you don't want to live like a peasant, shoving your neighbour's face into the bounty that you've managed to accumulate is a sure way to alienate just about everyone around you.

If you get homesick, go home for a visit before you drive everyone crazy.

When I first came to Ireland I didn't go back to the States for a visit for four entire years. To me, it seemed an eternity. Why, you may ask? Two reasons: first, I couldn't afford the airfare. Second, I thought that I needed to prove to everyone just how tough I was, and that I could live anywhere in the world with no problem.

Well guess what? I got homesick. And because of my overwhelming yearning for my homeland, those four years of self-deprivation nearly drove myself, and everyone around me, crazy.

Homesickness is akin to some sort of deadly poison that waylays the soul and seeks to destroy it. Homesickness can embitter a person. It can make life miserable and not worth living. It causes the sufferer to compare the far away pleasures of home with the ways of their newly embraced foreign lifestyle, and often with horrible results.

My memories of those first few years now seem embarrassing and almost silly. But in talking with other immigrants, I now realise that I was going through a fairly normal cycle of homesickness and feeling sorry for myself.

In short, my behaviour had become crazed.

A Survivor's Guide to Living in Ireland

For instance, I would drive out to the airport and spend a few hours wandering around the airport terminal. There, I would watch passengers bound for the United States, viewing them with a sense of overwhelming envy. I would pretend that I, too, was about to climb on a flight and in just a few hours I would be able to sink my teeth into a Big Mac (a ridiculous aspiration but in those days a McDonalds in Ireland was only a distant dream), or talk with distant friends, or simply stand with my feet planted on American soil.

On other occasions, I would make my way to Galway and out to the very tip of the Connemara peninsula. There, I would look out upon the Atlantic and wonder just how far west I could swim before sinking beneath those frothy waves. Though North America was a mere three thousand sea miles distant, hiding beneath the sinking sun, the thought that I could make that swim seemed almost certain. Needless to say, I had sunk into a fugue-like state of depression. Had I tried such a journey I obviously would not have made it far beyond the stony beaches of Galway's coastline.

Or another instance: in those early years, the sound of an American voice could drive me to distraction. Despite the loudness of their voices and the many-coloured clothes that they chose to wear, I was compelled on occasion to make my way toward any American tourist that had the grave misfortune to come within walking distance. My good wife would become annoyed and embarrassed as I interrupted these visitors' conversations with almost any excuse to make their company. I would ask about the state of the American economy, or about the last World Series, or what the price of a hotdog was at the local fast food joint. Anything at all would do. My occasional desire to seek people of my own kind, to smell them, to speak with them, to interact with them, helped me to remember that I was still American, despite the physical distance from my country. Upon seeing these pour souls, my homesickness would come to the surface like a submerged cork seeking daylight. The sight of Americans, my fellow countrymen and woman, only made my feelings of loneliness much worse.

As you can tell, being an immigrant can be confusing. On the one hand, you'll find yourself defending your new homeland (Ireland, in my case) to the hilt against any possible criticism. You will also attempt to minimise any ties that you might have with your old homeland and you'll do everything you can to truly believe that you have settled permanently in your new country.

On the other hand, you'll often find yourself illogically misty-eyed and patriotic about the country of your birth. In my case, and should an unsuspecting Irish person casually criticise the United States, I could go ballistic, defending to the death my country's right to do just about anything. Yet in the same breath, the other half of my brain would again begin to function, and I would start contradicting myself by criticising my country's actions simply because that other part of my psyche truly believed that our politicians just might be wrong.

In other words, the life of an immigrant can become dangerously schizophrenic. Don't be too worried about it if you are pulled apart at times by your emotions and the internal conflict that can arise. In talking with other immigrants, I've discovered that this state of absurd and often bemused confusion is absolutely normal.

But do take this piece of advice: if you get homesick make certain that you do something about it. Go home for a visit. Immediately. If you're from the Continent, buy a cheap ticket on Ryanair and taste again the life of Paris or Brussels or wherever you happen to be from. If from the States, cruise back to your hometown. Buy yourself a Big Mac if that's what you want to do. Take a stroll in the local Wal-Mart. Watch insipid American television.

Plant your feet on your native soil in order to reassure yourself that it hasn't gone anywhere, it's just that you don't happen to be living there anymore.

Then come back to Ireland. Take a big breath of clean air. Listen to the singsong voices of your neighbours. Buy yourself a pint of Guinness in your local. When you do, you'll find that life in Ireland isn't so bad after all.

Learn to drive on the other side of the road.

The Irish drive on the left hand side of the road. That means that the steering wheel is located on the right hand side of the car. If you happen to be from the U.K. you will, of course, find this the most natural thing in the world because you already drive cars on this side of the road. However, other people are not so fortunate. If you are from Continental Europe or the United States, do not be fooled into thinking that driving in this foreign manner is going to be simple. It is not and takes some getting used to.

Driving in Ireland is different. For one thing, you'll have to get used to roundabouts. Apparently, roundabouts were devised by an insane traffic engineer who thought that they might wreak havoc on unsuspecting motorists. Fortunately, roundabouts are only constructed in larger, more populated communities. But unless you plan to continue circling around them for the next hundred years or so, you'll need to learn to drive in them.

My early method was this: come to a stop ten metres or so from the roundabout. Wait for a gap to open in the traffic. Close eyes. Hit accelerator and hope for the best. Over the years I've improved on that method somewhat, though the initial methodology can still work and I have yet to have had a major accident in a roundabout.

In the early days of my driving in Ireland, how many times would I find myself turning down the wrong side of the road, gazing ahead only to find a large juggernaut bearing down on me with possibly terrifying consequences? Or, climbing into the car and looking up, wondering where the steering wheel had vanished to, then coming to the abrupt realisation that I'd sat (yet again) in the passenger seat and on the wrong side of the car?

Or reaching for the stick shift with my right hand and only finding the solid side of a door panel? Or looking for the rear view mirror on my right when it was firmly attached to the window frame on my left?

When you get to Ireland find yourself a School of Motoring. Every small town has one and you can get a list through the Golden Pages (our equivalent to the Yellow Pages). Within only a couple of lessons (each lesson costs approximately twenty euro – twenty-five bucks or so), you'll be driving in Ireland as if you'd been born there.

The alternative, of course, is to ask a friend or relative to teach you not only how to motor around a roundabout but also how to avoid turning onto the wrong side of the road. But employing a friend or relative for such a stressful task is only asking for trouble and could possibly lead to murder and dismemberment. A School of Motoring is the much better option.

A Survivor's Guide to Living in Ireland

Be open to the wonders around you.

I vividly remember the first time that I flew into Ireland. It was in December of 1980. As you now know, I had met my wife on a bicycling holiday only a few months earlier, and having proposed to her within a few days of our first meeting and then having gone back to the United States to find paid employment, had finally worked up the courage to board an Aer Lingus flight from JFK with the mission of marrying my newly found Irish bride.

As we flew toward Dublin airport, and it being winter, the sun rose late that day. But I remember the magic of that approach. We came into Dublin from the west, flying only a few thousand feet above vivid green fields and between cloud-scud that seemed to have been torn from the pages of a book on Irish Celtic fantasy.

Looking out the window, watching the tiny patchwork fields glow with the blood red of the rising sun, I thought that I'd never seen anything exuding such magic in my entire life.

If you move to Ireland you'll discover that magic for yourself. Ireland really is a place of magic. That magic may be a little more difficult to find today but it's still here. The country may now be awash with European money, U.S. multi-national companies, millions of cars, telephone systems that work, mobile telephones in every pocket, and five colour televisions in every home, but the ancient magic and folklore that have been at the core of this country for millennia is still here for anyone to see. You'll just have to look a little harder for it, that's all.

The magic of Ireland can be found in both its people and in the country that surrounds you. Try exploring any of the Gaeltacht areas – Gweedore in County Donegal for instance. Walking into a local pub you'll hear the locals speak in their ancient Irish and for a moment time will come to a standstill as you drink a pint and take a moment to smell the sweet smoke from the glowing peat fire.

Or drive through any county in the country – County Wicklow for instance. A twelfth century round tower will suddenly appear over the horizon looking abandoned and forlorn and seem anything but beckoning. But do yourself a favour: stop the car immediately and discover its wonders for yourself.

Unlike America, where each historical point of interest seems to come with its own forty-foot billboard, snack shop, tourist guide, and crowds of camera toting visitors, you may initially think that what seems to be an abandoned site only worthy of a wrecking ball wouldn't be worth visiting. If you think that way, you will be wrong.

Such sites of ancient Irish culture are fascinating and you could well have the place completely to yourself. With luck, you'll climb out of the car and that unique and never-to-be-forgotten mixture of recently expunged cow manure, clover and blooming heather will gently assault your senses. The quiet of the place may at first seem unnerving, but listen closely and you'll discover that your nervousness is the direct result of the fact that it *is* so quiet. You may hear the buzzing of bees or the lowing of sheep and cattle from a nearby farm, but that will be about it.

Then look up at the ancient, monumental round tower itself, poised like some stone-aged missile ready for lift-off, the grey of its thousand year old rocks covered with lichen, and you may experience what I have: through the mists you may swear that you could hear the calls of the local monks yelling in warning as the Vikings approach, swinging their battleaxes with killing on their minds, and watch as the good Brothers flee through ancient doors and up the steep spiral stairs in preparation for a bloody defence. The hairs on the back of my neck usually stand up, and I can swear that the ancient place whispers to me of its many secrets.

Ireland has so many magical places that it is pointless to even try naming them all in this one book. As an example of the historic booty that can lie within a stone's throw of almost anyplace you happen to live in this country, let me use my own area as an example.

Within a few minute's drive of my house, I can find some of Ireland's most fascinating national treasures: in Kells, a few miles north, rests the massive Cross of Kells. Its long dead stone carver brought alive a series of biblical passages, all ornately illustrated on its greying, rocky surface. In America, such a treasure would be locked away in a museum. Here, it shines with a steady magnificence from its outdoor location on the main Kells/Navan road, instantly accessible to anyone who chances by.

Or take the Newgrange Mound (or Monument) as another instance. Its immense bulk rises from the surrounding countryside like an alien spaceship. One face of it has been covered completely with white quartz that glitters knowingly in the sunlight. At its entrance, a huge rocky kerbstone, the shape of an immense lozenge, has been carved with ornate swirls, rectangles, and stony cups. Written on its surface may be an explanation of the purpose of the Newgrange Monument itself. However, and at over five thousand years old – older than the pyramids and possibly the oldest human engineered structure on the planet – that explanation has been lost forever. Once a year, and because of the delicate alignment of stones which the Old Ones raised so carefully, the rising sun lights the interior cavern with the glory of Winter Solstice thereby bringing hope that the winter might soon pass. This is a fantastic feat of ancient engineering and those lucky enough to witness it are truly blessed.

Within only a few hundred metres of this wondrous place lay Knowth and Dowth, sister mounds, and created by the same ancient engineers who developed Newgrange. While Dowth has not yet been completely examined by Irish scholars and is therefore closed to public scrutiny, the Knowth Monument has been completely rebuilt. Now open to the public, its multiple mounds and intricate stone carvings offer the visitor another example of the magic that exists in this fabled area of megalithic architecture.

Elsewhere, and only a few miles from my home, lie: Tara Hill, the ancient seat of the High Kings of Ireland; Slane Hill, upon which Saint Patrick is reputed to have lit the Paschal Fire thereby symbolising the coming of Christianity to Ireland; the King's Belly, a megalithic burial mound and located within the very perimeter of the town of Navan; Trim Castle, originally constructed in the 12th Century and which was – and still is – the largest Norman castle in the country.

The list goes on and on: castles, monuments, burial chambers, faery forts and ring forts, ancient abbeys and monasteries, mysterious standing stones and other magical structures that have been tossed like so much fairy dust only minutes from my front door. In the United States, many of these structures would have long ago been buried beneath cement-grey parking lots. Here, the ancient archaeological artefacts form a living historical fabric that is beyond written description.

Ireland is full of such magic. If you live here you'll have a chance to discover that magic for yourself. To do so, all you have to do is learn what many of us have never been taught: that reality isn't always what it seems, and that just beneath what our senses tell us lies a different world that perhaps – with a little luck – we may yet tap into.

De-construct your Nationalism before you do anything else.

The point of this chapter is this: while you may well be – and should continue to be – proud of your American, French, British, Norwegian, Canadian, Australian or whatever ancestry might happen to run through your veins, the things that you have learned and that you now value may actually inhibit your ability to settle happily in Ireland.

Ireland is a different country with a different culture and value system. It places less importance on how much money one earns and much more importance on what one knows and how one makes his or her way through life.

Success in Ireland is often measured not by the amount of cash one has in their bank account, but by the number of friends that a person has or the loyalty and courage a person has developed to face the difficulties in life.

For thousands of years, the Irish have faced innumerable challenges and despite everything have managed to overcome them. But the answers to their struggles have never been handed to them on a plate. The Irish have had to develop a sense of patience and humour that boarders on the impossible, and a dogged determination to overcome seemingly horrendous odds to achieve what may well have seemed unreachable.

If you immigrate to Ireland, this country offers you all of these values. You may not achieve the sort of financial success that has been set out for you in America or on the Continent; you may have to redefine your own expectations and unlearn what may have taken you years to understand.

But if you can start to develop a different view of yourself, if you can begin to appreciate your own person in a new light, then you stand a much better chance of settling here.

Guideline Nine
Despite Everything You'll be Criticised so Get Used to It

A friend of mine, another American expatriate, confided to me recently:

'I don't know about you, but since George W's decision to invade Iraq things have become more difficult. While most Irish realise that I am not personally responsible for American foreign policy, I can't help but feel that people are looking at me differently.

'Being an American living in a foreign land has always had its difficulties, but it's more troublesome now than it has ever been.'

Being a foreigner in a foreign land is difficult at the best of times. While immigrants to Ireland from Continental Europe, Britain, Canada, or other countries might find things a little tough, being American – particularly in the current political climate – can prove daunting. For a moment, I'll focus on the possible heartache that many American citizens face when immigrating to this country – or anywhere else, for that matter.

If you are American, and no matter what political party you belong to or what your stance is regarding current U.S. foreign policy, make no mistake that the present U.S. president, and his administration's policies, are going to have an impact on your life should you decide to live in Ireland or almost anyplace else in the world. You're going to have to get used to a new reality, a reality that has been the subject of countless books on the matter: many people, including a good few Irish, now dislike America with a passion that borders on hatred. That dislike can incorporate not only American foreign policy, but also everything that America stands for.

Unfortunately, there exist individuals who cannot, or will not, discriminate between our politicians' policies and ourselves, simple American expatriates though we are. For whatever reason American expatriates throughout the world have been caught in the crossfire of foreign hatred and distrust. Rightfully, those feelings should be directed at the U.S. Administration and not the American people. But occasionally – even in Ireland – those destructive emotions can be vented toward Americans who live abroad.

For instance, in early 2005 and less than one hundred miles north of my home in Navan, two American basketball players were beaten senseless by a group of Irish thugs. The Irish manager of the Irish basketball team for whom the Americans played made two points absolutely clear: first, that the American players had done nothing to incite the incident; second, that those who had beat up the players had done so for one reason only: their innocent victims were American.

In a few short years, and due in large part to America's foreign policy, American citizens living or visiting abroad have become the subject of ridicule and occasional displays of violence. And that is true even in Ireland. While you, dear reader, might agree with present U.S. policy it may prove positively disastrous to you or your family if you insist on shoving that policy down the throat of the average European. Many people on this side of the Pond disagree with U.S. and British intervention in Iraq. That opinion has been made known in marches throughout Ireland, England and much of the Continent. Thousands of European citizens – the Irish among them – took to the street to voice their discontent regarding a variety of U.S. policies. For instance, they disagree with current U.S. practices of holding prisoners in Guantanamo. They do not understand why the U.S. electorate has voted George W back into office; in fact they are positively disillusioned by the outcome of the 2004 election. In many cases, they now see America as a land of hypocrites who talk about liberty and justice on the one hand while simultaneously ignoring international law and international legal systems on the other.

It's enough to make many Americans cry. After all, we have been brought up to view ourselves as citizens of the most caring, most beneficent country on Earth. Most Americans, including many who live abroad, simply can't understand this new world viewpoint of our country or ourselves.

So what do we do about it?

The answer starts with some simple constructs: first, do your best to be open-minded. Second, try to appreciate the other side of the argument.

No matter what your opinion regarding current world affairs, Europeans including the Irish have a right to their own opinion. Moreover, that opinion just might be correct. As you know, the Irish have long been supporters of the United States. They recognise that America offered a haven of safety during the times of the Great Hunger. Moreover, they also understand that since then, and right up to the present day, America has been a land of opportunity for millions of Irish who have upped stakes and high-tailed it to the States in search of personal fortune.

But now, that almost instinctual decision to support America is under scrutiny. Due to its long history of occupation, the Irish have always leaned toward the side of the underdog. This time, America looks somewhat like a bully. And while many will agree that Saddam had to go and that the Iraqi's are infinitely better off without him, many Irish continue to question American (and British) policies and motives.

Many Irish side with those who believe the war in Iraq to have been motivated by oil interests. Too, many believe that the world was lied to and that the American government had no legal business invading Iraq in the first place. Add to this simmering mix a few other ingredients including the fact that the Irish government is supporting American policy by allowing U.S. military flights to refuel in Shannon Airport on their way to Baghdad, as well as the fact that the Irish government has never come out and directly stated that U.S. foreign policy is wrong (both actions being contrary to the opinion of much of their electorate) and things become a little tricky.

If you want to get on here the best thing that you can do is keep your mouth shut, grin and bear it, and try to listen and learn. You may not agree with what you hear, and you may well become angered by the hot opinions that will come flying toward you like a clutch of cruise missiles, but unless you desire to become the focus of mob rule it is best to at least pretend to an understanding of Irish opinion.

What's sad, of course, is the fact that many American expatriates have to suffer the slings and arrows of our country's foreign policy at all. After all, none of us has direct access to the Oval Office, do we? And whether we agree with the decisions made concerning Iraq, Guantanamo, Palestine, or any other foreign hotspot, many Europeans will associate American expatriates with these decisions, thinking that simply because we are American we also tacitly approve of U.S. policies and subsequent actions. Like America itself, the expatriate community is split on these issues, yet Americans abroad are all tarred with the same brush. But that's just the way of the world right now so you'd better get used to it.

But perhaps as difficult is the fact that if you stay out of the States long enough you will also have trouble understanding and communicating with your fellow Americans.

If you're gone from America long enough you will find it difficult to understand the situation at home, and the values and perceptions that your old friends, neighbours and relatives have. For instance, in my own case I find that I'm having great trouble relating to the present state of affairs in the United States, and the cultural divisions that are now so present in my native country.

The election and re-election of George W. Bush not only brought along tax cuts and the Iraq War but also deep fissures in the psyche of the American people. While America has always been distrustful of many segments of its own population (take race and civil rights issues for instance) I believe that America is probably more fractured now than at any other time since the Civil War. Today, Republicans distrust Democrats, the Christian Right distrusts liberals, abortionists distrust anti-abortionists, pro-War supporters distrust anti-War supporters...the list goes on and on.

At the root of that distrust lies a fundamental re-thinking of the very values that Americans hold to be the truth, as well as those behaviours that are acceptable within the context of those values. Consequently, great divides now run through the United States as people argue their positions with barely concealed – and often unconcealed – anger.

Below that anger, of course, is the fear that was planted in the country's people by the actions of September 11th. Americans are now afraid. That fear feeds the anger that in turn creates even more distrust as everyone searches for safety. And if you happen to be living abroad things can seem bewilderingly confusing because while you are an American you are not living in America and therefore are not directly involved in these burning discussions. Nor can you take part in, or truly appreciate, the various issues that these discussions centre upon. If you are gone many years, you simply cannot understand what people are talking about or why. All that you know is that people are angry and afraid which, in turn, brings about more confusion on the part of the expatriate.

Today, my problem isn't so much how to get along with those Irish and Europeans who disagree with American foreign policy, but rather how to get along and communicate with other Americans, my countrymen and women, whom I now no longer entirely understand.

A quick example: I am fortunate to have kept in touch with a number of American friends, usually by way of the Internet. In fact, some of those friends were responsible for this book in that they form part of the populace that kept asking me about the positives and negatives of living in Ireland.

Recently, an old acquaintance and I were having a discussion via Email about a topic that I now forget. For some reason or other I made a slight jab at President Bush. The remark went something like 'I think he's a nice guy and would be a great neighbour in that he probably makes a mean barbeque. But as a President? No way!'

This wisecrack to my friend was not made in anger. Nor was it in any way a reaction to something he had said (we never discussed politics prior to this). And that tiny sentence was written in earnest: I believe George W. Bush to be a nice enough human being. And I do think that he'd make a great and interesting neighbour. And I also suspect that he makes a mean barbeque (many Texans of my acquaintance really know how to get a steak just right and I'd love to learn their secret). And yes, I don't think that he should be the American President. In the last election, I voted for the other guy.

In times past, such a remark might generate a small amount of intelligent discussion, a trading of points of view, etcetera, etcetera, as both parties attempted to learn and grow from contrary opinion. But this time...oh, my! The reaction was as if a ballistic missile had been fired in my direction.

My acquaintance's subsequent Email was vitriolic, to say the least. He viewed my remark, made so innocently, as a personal attack on his values and his personal opinion of George W, whom he holds in high esteem. In closing he wrote,

'...you don't like President Bush...that is fine and you are entitled to not like him...but he is not your President since you don't live here...The US is a great country and one of the most generous, always the first to rush in to help. President Bush is still my President and I will treat him with the respect of the office as I have done with the Presidents before him.'

I was flabbergasted. In one short Email he had made it clear that a) my opinion was wrong, b) my opinion was disrespectful of the Office of the President of the United States, and c) my opinion didn't matter anyway because I no longer live in the United States.

Amazing.

But what is more shocking is my personal gut feeling that this person's attitude is held by many of my country-fellows. As far as many U.S. citizens seem to be concerned, expatriates have no inherent right to comment on U.S. policy, values, or behaviour simply because we no longer happen to live within the forty-eight contiguous States, Hawaii, or Alaska. Apparently, the Constitution of the United States makes little difference to these people. After all, I am still an American citizen, I still vote, I still pay U.S. taxes, and I still care not only what my country does, but also how my country fares. As the years go on my emotional ties to the U.S. have actually grown, not diminished.

Yet this makes little difference to those Americans who take a dim view of citizens who live abroad. I guess they figure that rather than love America, I left it. They have of course no understanding of why I moved abroad or what my current thinking is regarding this President and his policies. In that they are unlikely to read this book I doubt that they will ever come to such an understanding.

As importantly, they don't care about my opinion because – as with my acquaintance – my voice does not count.

It is an unfortunate state of affairs and it is, of course, my own fault. Because despite my own personal decision not to when I came to Ireland, I have changed. I am no longer entirely American. Instead I have been stretched by European and Irish thoughts and values, and my thinking and beliefs have changed because of that education. Some Americans might say that I've been brainwashed but I don't think so. Instead, I have unwittingly attended the College of New Insights. At this college I have learned that the American Way isn't the only way. Instead, it is just one of many that struggle to ensure that we make it through this life in one piece, and with a modicum of happiness.

If you decide to join the hundreds of thousands, even millions of other people from America and other countries who have chosen the life of an expatriate, be prepared for a learning process that can only result in personal growth. Your values and opinions will change. What you believe to be right and wrong will be tinged with a global viewpoint and expectations. You will learn to spell differently, talk differently, and interact with others in a manner peculiar to your adopted country. Invariably, but only if you are predisposed, your mind will be opened and a path made clear that will allow you not only to learn more about the attitudes, behaviours, and values of other nations and their peoples, but to appreciate those cultural aspects as well.

But at the same time, a part of you will continue to be rooted to your home nation.

This conflict of values – those that you have grown up with and those that you have learned – can lead to some strange happenings: there will be times when you will not only have trouble understanding the citizens of your adopted country, but your friends and family back at home as well. It can all result in some very disquieting experiences.

Being an immigrant in a new country is hard. Being an American immigrant in today's world is even harder. But despite the occasional confusion, frustration, and caustic remarks made to you by either the citizens from your immigrant country or back home, the journey is worth it.

It is worth it because we lucky immigrants have been given the opportunity that few other people are given: we can learn and grow by entirely submerging ourselves in a completely different culture. Immigration has always been part of the human experience. Historically, immigrants were most often driven from their home nations by economic disadvantage, prejudice, and similar plights to the human spirit. While these factors can still continue to drive immigration, today's immigrant often has a choice. Often, we move to new countries because we choose to. In doing so, we are presented with a tapestry of local culture from which we can truly benefit.

All we have to do is grasp the opportunity.

Guideline Ten
Come to the Ireland We All Love

Chicago, Illinois   *July 1, 2001*

My dearest Tom,

    Congratulations on your nineteenth year of living in Ireland and I'm delighted that you have managed to survive in that land of the ancient Celts. As for me...well, I've discovered that retirement isn't all it's made out to be. Robert has recently been made unemployed by his uncaring multi-national company and can no longer afford to make his mortgage payments. To my displeasure, he and his screaming wife are now living with me in my two-bedroom apartment and I can't possibly get a good night's sleep.

    Helen, my wife of thirty-five years, has run off with the used car salesman and the City Council is now tearing up the local park to make way for a new parking structure. My rheumatism is again acting up and I've discovered that my health insurance no longer covers the cost of medication – which will only set me back approximately five hundred dollars a month.

    Other than that things are great. I'm so glad that we've kept in touch all of these years. Do write when you have a chance.

Fondly as always,

Ronald

P.S. Would you mind if I came over for a visit next month? Do let me know if this would be convenient. I've already booked airline tickets but I will cancel them despite the high cost if you don't have room for me...R.

Living in Ireland has been a wonderful adventure, and despite the occasional temptation to bolt and run screaming back to the States I've always made the decision to stay. Time and again both friends and strangers have asked me not only why I moved here and why I choose to remain here but also what they should do when considering a similar journey.

If you have purchased this book you are undoubtedly considering, or dreaming of, a move over. I recognise that many factors may dissuade – or even prevent – you from achieving your dream. As outlined previously getting permission from the government to remain as a permanent resident (unless you are seeking political asylum, are married to an EU national, or have parents or grandparents who were Irish citizens) really is difficult.

It's also no secret that, depending on your skills and luck, getting a job here can sometimes seem as if it would require an act of God.

And there are any number of other factors that can occasionally drive me, or any expatriate, absolutely around the twist and that might give you pause to move to this country. I've already talked about some of those: the high cost of housing, the high level of taxation, the high price of just about everything.

Then, of course, there is the constant patter of rain. It seems to rain almost all of the time in Ireland. Of course, if it didn't rain the countryside wouldn't be green which would mean that the Irish government would have to change the colours of its national flag and Aer Lingus, the national airline, would have to completely repaint its fleet.

But it does rain. It rains constantly, persistently. It mists, drizzles, spatters, and buckets. Sometimes, usually in early May when you're thinking in your wisdom that spring must surely be on its way and that the rain will magically dry up and go away, the heavens open and the entire population begins to realise that the rest of their lives will be spent in dire need of therapy. And sometimes, it rains even longer. As I write this I note the date on my calendar: June 1st. And I look out the window. It's raining in miserable sheets, like a depressant's liquid nightmare.

The constant rain drives people to distraction. It's also one of the most important reasons why many Irish usually check out of here at least once a year and head for the Mediterranean or any other sunny climate in search of some much needed sunlight. Local holiday companies have grown rich because of the rainy plight of the Irish.

But despite the bad things – the prices and the rain, the government and the roads – I've stayed. I've stayed and I've prospered.

So why do I? Nothing is really preventing me from going home. To be quite honest there have been many times in the past twenty-something years when I've thought of chucking it all in and heading back to the bright lights of Los Angeles, Chicago or New York. As have my wife and children.

Yet here I am and here I'll stay. And for the following very good reasons:

The Medical System – like everything else, the Irish bitch and moan about it, especially when the government seems hell-bent on turning it into an under-funded monstrosity. I understand that the U.K.'s programme is under similar pressure, but I've also heard that many other European countries have superlative medical systems. While I can't compare the Irish way with other countries on the Continent (simply because I've never lived there), I have had the opportunity of comparing the Irish system with the American Way and I like what I see over here.

First of all it's pretty inexpensive. Yes, we pay high rates of taxes that are supposed to make it practically free, which it is decidedly not. But a stay in hospital won't turn you into a pauper by destroying whatever nest egg you've put by, as it will in the States if you don't have insurance.

But even though the Irish medical system is supposed to cost users a minimal sum, many Irish carry additional insurance cover in order to top-up standard benefits. In Ireland, medical insurance is offered primarily by two companies: BUPA and the VHI. Annual coverage (which can cost about fifteen-hundred euro – approximately two-thousand dollars – for a family of four) means that people will get immediate help in the event of something major going wrong, such as the need for a bypass operation for instance. You also get to stay in a plush single room rather than sharing the ward with other patients in need of medical help. But if you're willing to put up with waiting lists and don't mind sharing common facilities, insurance is unnecessary over here. If you don't have insurance the medical community will eventually get to you, be sure of it, but you'll have to wait in a queue. If your complaint is really serious, they'll do their best to get to you quickly.

However, standard medical costs are relatively small in comparison to the U.S. For instance, an emergency visit to the ER ('Casualty' on this side of the Pond) costs a mere twenty euro.

Prices for medical assistance, like everything else, have gone up however. In 1982, a trip to my local GP cost a whopping three Irish pounds – about five bucks. Today, the same visit to the doctor's surgery can set back a person suffering from a common cold fifty euro or a little more.

But despite rising prices the quality of care is still exceptional. Here's an example: a few months ago my mother came for a visit. She stepped off the airplane and to her misfortune became seriously ill. Within two days she found herself in hospital. My father – despite his change of attitude about the country – was decidedly unimpressed. The hospital looked seedy. It needed repainting. The beds looked as if they'd come out of a World War Two Army Surplus Store. He was worried that the quality of care would reflect the decidedly worn environment of the hospital ward.

He needn't have worried. The medical community here, at least for the most part, really gives a damn about their patients. Here, you are not a number but a real live human being. Doctors and nurses work hard to make sure that you stay that way. My mother spent three weeks in our local hospital and came out with a clean bill of health. My father was impressed. So was she, come to think of it.

Another example: my parents now live in Tampa Florida and unfortunately suffer from a number of medical complaints. Dad told me recently that if they didn't have appropriate medical insurance their meds would cost them over one thousand bucks a month. I couldn't believe it.

Here, on the other hand, we have a drugs scheme. If, say, one of the kids gets sick we go to our pharmacist ('chemist' in Ireland) and buy the necessary prescriptions. Each month we pay a maximum of eighty-five euro for drugs. Anything over that is paid for by the government.

If Mom and Dad lived here, and though the actual cost of their drugs might be one thousand dollars a month, they would only pay the maximum, or eighty-five euro a month. Not bad.

Yet another example: recently, my daughter became ill. Our family doctor, afraid that she might get worse by coming out into the cold and damp, made a house call. Yes, *a house call*. They still have them over here. This is just another example of the care that we are fortunate enough to receive in this part of the world.

It is true that because of the relatively small size of our population the medical community here does not have access to some of the most recent procedures that you may have access to in the States, Britain, or on the Continent. While this country is rapidly becoming wealthy it still has a far way to go to fix the problems that have plagued it since the middle of the seventeenth century. But most established procedures – such as heart surgery, transplant surgery, cancer therapy, and similar – are not only available here, but are carried out by well-trained, professional, and caring surgeons and staff. If I ever become critically ill I will have the confidence of knowing that these people really are concerned about my welfare. And even when I'm old and grey, I will know that in the eyes of the Irish medical community I am not dispensable. They will care for me with the same consideration as anyone half my age, and who might have another lifetime to live.

The School System – if you have younger children, I suspect that you'll fall in love with the school system here. Just like I did. While I have already spoken at length about Ireland's fantastic college and university system, let me spend a little time talking about its primary and secondary education programme.

Initially, you'll be shocked by the lack of school infrastructure. Because of the historic under-funding of the Irish education system, many children are still taught in schools that can seem to date back to the turn of the century. The vast majority of schools don't have those fun emoluments that many Americans or Europeans might be used to: they don't have an indoor pool. They don't have a theatre. They don't have an indoor gym with thousands of bucks worth of weight lifting equipment. Instead, PhysEd is usually conducted in a multi-purpose room that can often double as the school's cafeteria.

But despite the alien looking infrastructure the quality of education is outstanding and the kids benefit from it in every way. Here, educators still concentrate on Reading, Writing and 'rithmatic. When graduating from school, Irish kids know how to read, write, add and subtract. They have sound foundations in science and the arts. They are not subjected to newfangled ways of education nor are treated as guinea pigs and subjected to methods that *might* improve the learning process and which you will only be in a position to judge when your offspring fail to achieve a satisfactory Leaving Certificate, SAT or A Level score.

The majority of Irish teachers are good. They are patient. They know what they have to do. As importantly, they are still respected by the community. Irish teachers know that they are still involved in a proud profession. Unlike in the U.S., it is still a job of work that many aspire toward.

Irish schools operate differently from those in the States and much of the rest of the world. Kids usually go to school at the age of four, attending a year of Junior Infants followed by a year of Senior Infants. This is sort of equivalent to America's kindergarten.

Following that, they enter Primary School. Kids attend for six years. Then the fun really starts. Upon graduation they enter Secondary School.

Secondary School combines U.S. middle school and High School. Students attend for six years and may have an option of attending a seventh year – or transition year – that occurs following their third year. During transition year many students will work on special projects, set up a small business, or work in the community.

By the way, and for the benefit of American readers, kids in Secondary School don't call themselves Freshmen, Sophomores, Juniors or Seniors as they make their way through the years. Their progress is tracked simply by the year in school: you're a First Year Student, or Second Year, or Third, etc.

Secondary School is a real trip because students come under incredible pressure in that they know from the very beginning that at the end of their schooling they must sit what is known as their Leaving Certificate Exam. The Leaving Cert, which assesses them in all of their subjects and which they sit during one entire week of hell, causes headaches, insomnia, and nervous breakdowns not only for the students but also for their parents.

Let me explain.

Most Europeans or peoples from other global communities will understand this examination procedure. But for Americans, it will be a completely foreign concept – rather like a pressure cooker from which students hope to escape unscathed. In the U.S. as you know successful college entrance is determined by a number of assessments: your high school grade point average, your SAT and

ACT scores, and perhaps an interview or essay that is submitted to the college or university at the time of application. Here it works much differently.

While kids take exams throughout their secondary school years this sort of continual assessment has nothing to do with whether or not a student makes it into the college of their choice. Neither do Irish kids take an SAT or ACT multiple-choice exam or their equivalent, nor do they submit an essay.

Rather, they sit their Leaving Cert. This one series of exams – one exam for each subject that they've studied – is the whole Chihuahua. During this single exam week they are assessed on their entire six years of Secondary School education. Kids receive points (somewhat the equivalent to the U.S. grade point average) in relation to how well they do on each exam. The better they perform, the more points they receive. The points from all exams are then totalled.

They submit their point totals to Ireland's Central Applications Office, or the CAO, which is a centralised clearinghouse of sorts that has been set up to process college applications. As part of their submission, the students also provide their preferences regarding college and major. Then the race is on.

Kids who have enough points make it not only into the college of their choice but also into their preferred major. Kids who don't have enough points for their first preferences must make do with something else: either their secondary choice of college or university, their secondary choice of major, or both.

Some unfortunates with low point totals don't make it in at all. These kids can either say to hell with it and get a job, or re-sit the Leaving Cert in hopes of achieving a better point total.

During the Leaving Cert season this country thrums with a feeling of tension that I've never seen anywhere else. Is it any wonder that some parents make sure that they've secreted away a week's supply of Prozac for themselves (not their offspring!) prior to the examination?

Perhaps this system is unfair. I'm not sure. I do know that if I had to go through the process I probably would never have made it into college. Here, kids who deal with pressure and who sit exams well are more likely to get through the exam nightmare in one piece, and achieve a higher points total, than those who don't.

This means that some talented kids who don't perform under pressure are left behind. Irish parents and certain government agencies including the Irish Department of Education are aware of this problem and rumours abound that the college entrance process – including the Leaving Certificate examination requirement – may well change. But for now, students planning to matriculate into Irish colleges and universities are stuck with it.

But despite the system's few shortcomings I do know one thing. Irish kids are renowned for their intelligence, dedication, and quality of education. They are recognised for the foundation that they have in academic fundamentals. That's one reason why the likes of Microsoft, Intel, IBM, and a host of other American and European companies have set up shop here. They come, at least in part, for the talent and the quality of Irish education.

Television – yeah, I know, what the hell does television have to do with the decision to come to Ireland? I realise that it shouldn't matter but to me it matters very much indeed. For you see, I have come to hate American television (though I must admit a certain fondness for *Desperate Housewives*, which we have just begun to receive, but that's a different story). U.S. television production companies and broadcasters must think that the entire population of America is dense. If not, why do they insist on creating inept programming that could only possibly interest a chimpanzee? It makes no sense.

As mentioned elsewhere in this book I can't say that I like the local broadcaster's efforts that much either. RTE executives surely must have to take courses in such interesting and worthwhile subjects as 'Dumbing Down the Irish Populace' in order to land their highly paid jobs. This might explain the incredibly stupid and ignorant TV programmes that they create.

Of course they can't create enough of this absolute rubbish to fill all of their broadcasting slots. So what do they do? They import American absolute rubbish. But fortunately most Irish people have a secret weapon.

We can view British television – and what makes it even more pleasurable is the fact that we can do so for free! That's right, folks. In that the BBC, ITV and Channel Four allow their signals to beam well beyond their shores many of us in Ireland can pick up said signal without having to pay even one penny in additional television licence fees. What a boon!

No matter where in the world you live, you're probably aware of some British programming because a wide variety of global cable stations occasionally buy their outstanding wares. British television is, for the most part, wonderful. Their drama is great. Their documentaries superb and intelligently crafted. Their news programming, unlike much U.S. and Irish television news, tries valiantly to be impartial and usually succeeds.

In that we have purchased SKY satellite programming, the Richards are now able to avail of a whole stream of British treats. My wife watches *Coronation Street* – the longest running soap in the history of the world – three nights a week and I hate to say it but I've also become caught up in the stories of this series' convoluted characters.

We also love to watch any number of documentaries that are rich in content, information and astounding in their choice. They are created for one real purpose: while they might entertain, they also educate. What a wonderful mission!

We enjoy a hospital drama series entitled *Casualty*. It's the U.K.'s version of *ER* but without the histrionics or shaky and distracting hand-held camera work. And we love the endless mini-series that are made in Britain. The British have a wealth of history and they use that as the foundation for their imaginations. Their creativity finds its way into stories that are rich in entertainment, fact, and fantasy.

If I had to go back to the U.S. I probably wouldn't buy a television at all. Instead, I'd either immerse myself in a series of good books or – if I were lucky – I'd give in and buy that telly but only if I could figure out how to beam in the wonderful television from Britain.

The People – what is it about the Irish people? After all of these years, they can still be an enigma to me and can often drive me around the twist. When asked a favour they rarely say no, nor do they say yes, but rather keep you hanging on the question; they often keep up a ruse of ignorance rather than letting you know up-front that they happen to have a doctorate in philosophy and could talk rings around you.

But the Irish really are the most welcoming people in the world. However, if you come to live here things obviously change a bit. When I initially immigrated to this country I thought that what you see is what you get: big smiles, hearty welcomes, firm handshakes. Needless to say, I soon discovered that behind the welcoming veneer the Irish are far more complex than first appeared.

History has much to do with this complexity, as it does with most any nation of peoples. The Irish were subjugated by their English rulers for hundreds of years. To survive they learned to adapt to constant suffering and the yoke of terror. The Irish learned early on to keep their friends close and their enemies closer. To do so they may chat about the inconsequentials of life but what they are really doing is weighing you up, deciding what you really are and if you are worth their time. If you pass the test the Irish will adopt you as one of their own.

The Irish people are neat. Behind a smokescreen of provincial blarney they prove to be warm hearted and caring. This is born out by the fact that the peoples of this island contribute more per capita to charities than any other country in the world. They will take time out from their busy schedules for a chat and spend a couple of hours over a cup of tea expounding about your wife's Great Aunt who is suffering from an incurable malady and what a wonderful life she has had, God be good to her. And they will also take time out just to listen to you.

I love the Irish despite their warts.

In my opinion the Irish still have a sense of what is valuable in this world. Yes, like many of us, some can be sadly motivated only by money – and have adopted an underlying sense of greed – as has any other first world culture. Recently, and as in many other nations, some Irish have lost one of their most reliable anchors as the Catholic Church, struggling with lies, lechery and deceit, has imploded. It's sad to say but Ireland is fast losing its sense of innocent spirituality that has been part of this culture since time began.

But despite all of this the Irish still seem to embrace one critical value: people are important.

Because of this the Irish have some interesting characteristics: while family sizes are falling (until recently, the Irish had some of the largest families anywhere) those families continue to be incredibly important to them. This attitude was enshrined in legislation: for instance, only in the past few years has it become possible to obtain a divorce. However, a divorce is only granted following four years of legal separation. Consequently, warring husbands and wives are given every opportunity to kiss and make up.

Children are revered by Irish society. They are not the only peoples who feel and behave this way, of course. Like the Greeks, Portuguese, and other cultures, Ireland's folks place their children at the centre of their nation. They spend millions in caring for their children by supporting great education. They have instituted a Children's Allowance in which each month every family receives a lump sum of cash based on the number of children in a given family, which is to be spent by that family on their children. Poorer families receive government financial help for the purchase of everything from shoes to Confirmation dresses.

This attitude of care extends right down to how we look after each other's progeny. When my kids were small, and if I took one of them in a stroller to the local shopping centre, complete strangers would offer to look after my daughter or son should I have a sudden call to nature. The best thing about it was the fact that I could completely trust these people, knowing that my children would come to absolutely no harm, and might possibly enjoy the few moments of surprising company.

While the Ireland of today has changed somewhat, and though the culture of this country has become wary of the stranger, this child-centric attitude continues to exist. It comes to the fore when things go wrong.

Only a few days ago, in May 2005, a school bus loaded with over fifty kids that were being transported home from my town of Navan's secondary schools was involved in an accident. Many of the children were injured, six critically. Tragically, five fine young girls – four of them from a school that my daughters attended – lost their lives. The outpouring of grief stretched to the far corners of this country as people realised what had happened. That grief was real.

When the bodies of the young women were laid to rest, Navan literally closed down. Thousands attended the funeral Masses.

Messages of condolence came from every city, town, and small village in this country. The Irish people realised that they had lost five individuals who were the future of this country, and who represented the best of Irish society.

It was a tragic event. But once again it illustrated to me just how closely to their hearts the Irish hold their children.

The Irish are wonderful. They are surprising, intelligent, knowledgeable, clever, and capable. They make good neighbours, bosses and friends. When they have the time, they'll spend more hours nattering across a fence than almost any group of people that I know. If you are in trouble, as I have been in the past, they will do almost anything to help if it's in their power to do so. And if it's not, they'll do what they can to sort it out despite the fact. The warmth of these people, perhaps more than anything else, keeps me here and for one very good reason. They have adopted me as one of their own.

The Countryside – a 'soft' day in Ireland is unlike any other day anywhere else in the world. By a 'soft' day, I mean one full of gentle rain…a mist that tickles your cheeks and gets in through the lining of your coat. Yes, it makes things damp. But it makes it wonderful, too.

Taking a walk through the Irish countryside on such a day is an incredibly fulfilling experience. The world seems to lie under a velvet glove that squishes beneath footfalls of low-lying grass. Sheep bleat softly as they graze in a nearby meadow. Small purple flowers, defying gravity and covered by tiny sapphire water droplets, grow from the cracks in worn rock walls that are certain to be more than three hundred years old.

It's magic and difficult to describe unless you've been here.

Last year, for instance. I'd just finished a two-hour workout at a Yoga class conducted by my guru, another American expatriate. We walked out of the building – in this case a nineteenth century Great House that a local nunnery now owns and within which they occasionally permit the likes of us to congregate – and took a seat on the low stone steps that ran in front of the building.

We were sweating like pigs. My Yoga instructor can sometimes be a monster, and she had taken great joy in seeing her charges suffer through a painful workout that evening. But now the work was finished.

For a long time we just sat, saying nothing. It was after ten in the evening but it being summer the sky still reflected a soft glow from the setting sun. Countless green fields swept like a thick carpet in front of us. The air was full of the fragrance of mid-summer flowers, and we could hear the distant call of a bovine critter calling to its mate as it made its way home.

I looked at my friend. At that point she had been living in Ireland for four years. Every now and then she talked to me about going home. Like me, she often wondered what's greener: the sparkling excitement of America, or the green grass that stretched at her feet.

'Are you still thinking of going back to the States?' I asked her.

'Well,' she said, breathing deeply of the tranquil air. 'Maybe not right now.'

Maybe not forever.

A strange force keeps me captive in this country. It is something that I do not entirely understand, and it is something from which I do not particularly want to escape. In these often fraught and maddening modern times Ireland can seem a pleasant, mystical anomaly.

In Navan, living as we do in the Boyne Valley, the sense of the mystical is close at hand. The countryside is a patchwork of secret places littered with ancient monuments. Around every corner medieval castle keeps, round towers and falling down fortresses confront those with a keen eye. Faery rings, magical circles of trees that are said to be populated by the Auld People – the living ghosts of the Tuath de Danaan, the original peoples of Ireland – abound. Small round hillocks that are the up-thrusts of megalithic burial mounds, the surviving markers of those who lived here so long before us, grow unmolested in the middle of deserted farmers' fields.

Within the circumference of only a few miles we have some incredible wonders at our fingertips: the five thousand year old burial mound of Newgrange, that fabulous hillock built of ancient stone and quartz, casts its magical spell only ten short miles from my front door. The Hill of Slane, where it is said that Saint Patrick once lit the Pascal Fire resides in the town by that same name and is located just up the road from us.

Five miles or less as the crow flies from my home rests the Hill of Tara. This ancient seat of the High Kings of Ireland, crammed with overgrown ditches, dykes and foundations dug thousands of years ago, fills one with a sense of awe even though it is now nothing more than a large green field perched on a hill overlooking the valley below. It has been a holy place since time immemorial. Druids are said to have prayed to their gods of nature on this high windswept hill, and walking through the grassy tufts I swear that I can hear the whispering voices of their ancient indulgences at my back.

Last June the twenty-first, on Summer Solstice, and accompanied by my wife and son, we visited the Hill of Tara and took part in an ancient revelry that goes back thousands of years. Hundreds of people were there, many from as far away as France, Spain and, yes, America to join in the midsummer's night celebrations.

As the sun sank over the horizon a simple brazier was lit. A group of local actors took on the parts of ancient Druids to give thanks for the goodness of this country and the peace of life that can be found here. We looked to the North, East, South and finally to the West where the sun was setting over a far horizon, and we joined in a prayer of thanksgiving.

And as the light of the fire flickered its golden shadows over the people of Ireland, I looked at my family and I too gave thanks for the good fortune that had brought me to this fair country in the first place.

Guideline Eleven
Holidays. Learning to Love Them Like the Irish

Chicago, Illinois   *January 1, 2002*

Dear Tom,

Happy New Year and I hope that you had a wonderful and restful holiday period. In that I have been unable to pay for my incredibly expensive medication I have had no choice but to re-enter the educational workforce, and am once again ploughing the furrow in hopes of making a desperate living.

While I must say that I don't particularly enjoy the job anymore, it does have its benefits. For instance, I receive plenty of time off due to the fact that the schools close over the Christmas period. I'm so very lucky, and I know that all Americans are. While we may not get as many days off as you do, we still find time to buy the presents, cook the turkey, make the pies, and even wash out our underwear between trips to and from work.

Robert rang last night. Having finally landed another job (he has at last moved out of the apartment), he called to tell me just how fortunate he has been this year. He managed to get Christmas Day off! What a treat. Of course, he had to go back to work the next day, but he was delighted by his good fortune.

You wrote that you really do enjoy your Irish holidays. Do please explain. I cannot fathom a Christmas spent outside the United States and without the benefit of the various college and professional football games. Happy Holidays,

Ronald

If I ever have to go back to the United States and live there permanently I will never again be able to become gainfully employed simply because I have been spoiled by an Irish institution that every man, woman and child looks forward to on an annual basis: the Christmas Break.

Christmases, as with every other aspect of this country, have changed significantly over the years. When I first arrived in this country, Christmas was much more of a spiritual and religious holiday than it is today for the simple reason that no one had any money. Consequently, people might give only a single gift to each other but it was the spirit with which it was given that counted, not the monetary value. And in my opinion, that's how it should be.

With the advent of the Celtic Tiger, and the addition of vast wads of disposable income to their lives (or a multitude of over-charged credit cards), at Christmastime the Irish now do what most Americans, British, and other Europeans do: they run down to their local shopping centre, shop until they drop, and spend an incredible fortune that will only be paid down sometime in the following millennia. Unfortunately, and unless you happen to own a department store and thereby benefit from the crazed process of removing hard-earned cash from other people's pockets, spending at Christmas in Ireland has become big business.

Other holidays have their own Irish signature stamped on them: Halloween and Saint Patrick's Day, together with the Summer Holidays, are only some of the reasons why I enjoy living here so much. Let me try to help you experience living through a year of such times just so you know what you're missing, and what you could gain by moving here.

Christmas

What I love about Christmas in Ireland, and what I would miss should I ever go back, is rather straight-forward to report: the incredible amount of time we get off here.

Over the Christmas period, and unless you happen to be employed in the retail trade (in which case you'll be working right up until Christmas Eve and possibly can't stand the thought of another Christmas), most of the country's business infrastructure comes to a virtual standstill as it closes down. During that period of Christmas holiday magic – which can last for as long as two and a half weeks, from the middle of December through New Year's and beyond – the Irish go crazy as they begin to prepare for this time of family celebration.

During this period, I particularly enjoy putting my feet into the glowing coal fire and bemoaning the fate of my American friends, many of whom only receive both Christmas Day and New Year's Day off as the sum total of their Yuletide holiday period. And while I still miss celebrating Thanksgiving with my American family – and no, the Irish don't celebrate Thanksgiving in that that day of gratitude is a decidedly North American affair – we try to make up for it. Every year of our marriage my good wife Bernie has done her best to put a complete Thanksgiving spread on the table including a turkey and all of the trimmings. So while I don't get to see a live broadcast of the Macy's Thanksgiving Day Parade, at least I'm stuffed to the gills by the end of the day, so I don't particularly mind.

In our house, the Christmas period usually starts in the third week of November when Bernie puts together the Christmas Pudding. This amazing concoction, made of breadcrumbs, mixed fruit, a half bottle of Guinness, and a few tumblers of Irish whiskey for added flavour, has been handed down to her from her mother Kathleen, who in turn received it from her mother, and so on and so forth and into ancient history.

All of the ingredients are poured into one large bowl and mixed into a batter the consistency of tar. In turn, the batter is split and poured into two smaller bowls of an elegant shape, which are finally turned into a huge pot of boiling water. There, they bubble away for hours and hours and the house is filled with the smells of spices and fruits and a little homely magic. Everyone holds their collective breath when Bernie finally lifts the finished Puddings from the pot. It's akin to a scene from the *Christmas Carol* as we wait to see if the Puddings have been properly boiled, or if they will fall asunder in a mass of half-baked breadcrumbs. But for all of our married life, the Puddings have always come out perfectly. They sit in our larder, growing even tastier as the whiskey and Guinness combine to turn the two-pound'ers into alcoholic-tinged Christmas treats, and I must wait until the Christmas Season is really upon us in order to be allowed to imbibe.

As November passes the country shifts up a gear. Christmas decorations and magnificently presented presents of shaving lotions, potted plants, and chocolates that might be just the thing for Uncle Michael or Aunt Anna have been sitting in the shops since late October but now the Irish fly into a mad maelstrom of shopping that can leave me breathless.

They spend and spend and spend, buying everything and anything: chocolate covered nuts that seem to burst from their packaging saying please eat me; huge bushy poinsettias hallowed with red or white leaves that will be placed on windowsills or around fireplaces for that special seasonal touch; twenty speed bikes for junior that he will use to demolish the front garden; brightly coloured, elegantly presented dresses created only for that special holiday party; holiday wreaths composed of fragrant pine or waxy forest leaves of deepest green holly that will be hung on doors or used to adorn the gravesites of long-lost relatives who reside up at the local Cemetery; books of all types that talk of Irish poets or saints or writers that will sit quietly on some out of the way coffee table until there is nothing left to do but read them; and wax-made angels and small porcelain snowmen that decorate even the smallest corner in festive glory.

As the days pass and the deepest part of the season approaches, it also grows darker. Winter solstice bears down on us and the sun retreats even further, seeming to have abandoned the country in a dismal gloom. Going to work can be a trial: in mid-winter, the sun sets at the miserly hour of four-thirty in the afternoon and keeps its head down until almost 8:00 AM. This means that few of us working stiffs know what our homes look like for a good part of the year. But the Irish make up for this dark imprisonment by lighting welcoming coal and turf fires that keep the cold out and turn many a living room into a boiler house of cheer. Outside, the Irish have imported the custom of their American cousins and many a home is made even more cheerful with multi-coloured fairy lights that turn the towns and villages of Ireland into sparkling magic.

A few days before Christmas, depending upon the year that's in it, the country's employed population says goodbye to their colleagues and comes home for the long winter break. Cars are parked resolutely in front of homes and possibly won't be moved for another few weeks. Last minute shopping gets started and the storefronts along the main streets are packed with eager purchasers determined to make this the best Christmas ever. All of these goodly people march home with a spring in their step, loaded down as they are with goodies for what seems to be the entire nation.

Now all of the Christmas trees go up, bought as they have been from the local fruit merchants that also stock them, crammed into the boots of cars as they hurry home to deck their own halls in holiday cheer. With Christmas finally upon us, and the shopping almost done, everyone settles into a joyous quietude filled with expectation.

And finally, it is Christmas Eve. The night is dark and often damp, and the Irish light a candle in their windows, welcoming the Christ Child to the warmth of their homes. The people then turn out to Christmas Eve Mass in all of their finery, and the churches of Ireland are packed out with those who choose to give thanks to a God that has brought prosperity to their country, and to whom they can now worship freely. Following Mass, many will go home to put their houses in order. But many revellers choose to find the nearest pub and there celebrate with a quiet pint or a warming hot whiskey made fragrant with cloves and sweeter still with the addition of spoonfuls of castor sugar.

My favourite time is late that night. The roads are almost deserted. We might take a walk through our estate, enjoying the chilly silence, listening to the tolling bells of the distant church echo through the holy night, absorbing the quiet glow of golden candles standing like welcoming sentries in many a window, and sensing the comforting joy of another Irish Christmas.

Then, finally, it's off to home and the quietude of Christmas Eve.

Christmas Day itself is a time spent with family and friends. There's not much else to do anyway because every shop in the country is closed on that day. Gifts are exchanged. The Christmas turkey is prepared and stuffed to the gills with breadcrumb stuffing. The Christmas Ham is taken from its wrapper, washed, and placed into the warm oven or in a waiting pot. Potatoes, carrots and parsnips are peeled and placed in their boiling vessels, there to bang noisily as if wanting to get out.

When everything is ready, these ingredients are massed onto plates like small mountains: first a slice of ham. Then a spoonful of stuffing. The carved turkey laid on top of that. Then a few foothills of mashed potatoes, possibly a couple of roast potatoes, a spoonful of peas, a measure of carrots and parsnips (mashed together and enjoying their new harmony very much), and over it all a gallon of turkey gravy.

Next to our plates rest the Christmas Crackers, those small brightly presented festive tubes that hold miniscule surprises and that help to give even more merriment to the day. Each reveller picks one up, holding an end as their neighbour takes the other. As they pull, the Cracker finally relents to the stress, gives a resounding 'Pop!', and surrenders the undersized treats that have been hidden within. Each Cracker comes with an assortment of small gifts that people haggle over throughout the rest of the dinner: miniature scissors, tiny ornaments, games, and even little books. It's serious business, this cracking of the Christmas Cracker, and the diners will play with their little games as they also pour more gravy onto their mountainous meals.

The Crackers also hold two items that are fundamental to an Irish Christmas: first up is the joke. These absolutely horrid lines are written on a strip of paper possibly no larger than those that are held by any Chinese Fortune Cookie. One after another, each dinner guest must read their joke, the object being to discover who has the worst written, and the revellers practically fall over as they laugh and guffaw at each other.

The final item of each Cracker is the paper hat. Coming in different colours, and of the 'one size fits all' variety, these ridiculous crepe paper items must be worn by all in order to prove just how ridiculous they really are to the world. It works in that everyone wear them – even my mother-in-law when she was still with us – and for a moment at least the child comes out in each of us as we laugh uproariously at each other's stylish new look.

Having gorged ourselves on the piles of turkey and ham, taking the decision to clean up later in the day, and with everyone overstuffed and not able to eat another thing, the Christmas Pudding and Christmas Cake are brought out and the poor population is encouraged to eat just a little more because of the day that's in it. The Christmas Cake, by the way, is a sort of fruity concoction made of raisins, mixed fruit peel, and other savoury delights held together by darkened flour made rich with a mixture of treacle and sugar, and over which a blanket of hard icing has been lovingly trawled.

A Survivor's Guide to Living in Ireland

Having laid a huge section of Christmas Pudding and Christmas Cake side by side on a china plate, many pour a large dollop of fresh cream, hot custard, or – my favourite – a great mound of brandy butter on top of these seasonal creations hoping to hide the high calorie content below.

Glass of brandy in hand, we now pile this mass of sweet on top of a stomach already bulging from the above-mentioned meal. Finally comatose, we sit for the rest of the day in large overstuffed chairs that match the countenance of our constitutions, watching mindless television and pretending that we have not fallen asleep.

But still the holiday is not ended because the next day is Saint Stephen's Day! This day, which is technically the celebration of the first Christian martyr, has little to do with the Saint and much more to do with taking it easy. However, one group of people are still hard at work: the Wren Boys.

This 'Day of the Wren' harkens back to ancient Celtic mythology which suggests that the Robin – who represented the new year and the coming spring – would peck the poor Wren – a bird symbolising the old year and the winter's chill – to death. Since ancient times, the Wren Boys would darken their faces, dress in a variety of black or mysterious clothing, and go from door to door begging for money with which to bury the newly departed Wren. If they should come to your door, they might sing the following:

> The wren, the wren, the king of all birds,
> On St. Stephen's Day was caught in the furze,
> Although he is little, his family is great,
> I pray you, good landlady, give us a treat.
>
> My box would speak, if it had but a tongue,
> And two or three shillings, would do it not wrong,
> Sing holly, sing ivy – sing ivy, sing holly,
> A drop just to drink, it would drown melancholy.
>
> And if you draw it of the best,
> I hope in heaven your soul will rest;
> But if you draw it of the small,
> It won't agree with these wren boys at all.

If they should suddenly show up at your house the best thing to do is reach deep into your pocket and like the song says hand them at least a few bob if you know what's good for you. Otherwise the poor dead Wren will never get a proper burial, nor will the thirsty lads get a drink. In that the pubs are open on St. Stephen's Day, that's exactly what they have in mind and why they trudge through the winter's cold singing a song that stretches back to times immemorial.

However, Christmas still isn't over. I am delighted to say that the season lasts another few weeks, right up to Little Christmas on the 8th of January, which celebrates the occasion of the Magi bringing gifts to the Christ Child of Gold, Frankincense and Mir. Thankfully, we don't have to exchange gifts on that day, and a good thing it is too, because by that point everyone in Ireland is stony broke.

Christmas in Ireland is a time of magic marked by a pre-Christmas period of frantic shopping, incredible cooking, and enough drinking to sink even the largest of vessels. While it has become commercial here, just as elsewhere in the world, an Irish Christmas is still a time for family and friends; a period of quiet reflection; a breather in the year in which we all thank our lucky stars that we're still alive and kicking.

If you come here you too can take part in an Irish Christmas. It's a holiday that I heartily recommend.

Hallowe'en

Did you know that many Irish, despite these fast-paced modern times, still believe in ghosts and things that go bump in the night? It's true, you know. And at no time is that belief more telling than on Hallowe'en night.

I happen to enjoy this holiday, celebrated as it is in Ireland. There's something wonderfully creepy about the entire affair, a time of dark magic that has not yet been borne off by the commercialism that now surrounds the American celebration. On Hallowe'en night, the dark forebodings of ancient Irish mythology seem to creep out from every darkened corner and hidden floorboard.

A Survivor's Guide to Living in Ireland

The Irish love a good ghost story tinged with horror and suspense and that's exactly what you get on this night. Years ago, during my wife's childhood, Hallowe'en was a time of dark fun. At that time, only thirty years ago or so, pumpkins weren't available in this part of the world. Yet the Irish still had a ghostly way of marking the celebration: they would carve out a turnip, turning it into an image of spectral magic. If you have never seen a turnip – and I hadn't until I came here – you would be shocked at the amount of work it takes to carve a simple lantern from this obstreperous vegetable. Round, but packed as densely as a carrot, my father-in-law would take a knife to it, carving out its innards and creating a spooky face that would later be lit by a candle.

Meanwhile, Ireland's boys would go in search of any burnable rubbish that they could find in order to create the immense Hallowe'en bonfire that would be the highpoint of the celebration. For weeks before Hallowe'en night you could find lads loaded down with old tyres, furniture, wooden pallets, newspapers, and anything else that they could find and that might possibly burn, carrying all of this rubbish into a deserted field, and finally stacking it in a huge mound (at times, more than twenty feet high) that would be lit on that dark night.

Back before I came here, Hallowe'en night itself was marked with small parties, tricks, ghostly stories and innocent mischief. When it turned dark the kids of the neighbourhood would sneak to each other's house, there to play 'Knick-Knock'. Essentially, they'd bang the hell out of the front door, thereby rousing the occupant within from certain sleep, then run away pell-mell, finding some dark corner as they watched the homeowner stand at the front door with a worried expression on his or her face.

Or they would steal front garden gates. At that time, many of the small houses (including my tiny Navan house) had fences of wrought iron that cordoned off each small front garden, one from the other. Each fence also held a wrought iron gate through which one could gain access to their home. Those gates were held down only by gravity and a series of simple hinges.

On Hallowe'en the kids would snatch the gate, laughing like Satan as they ran into the black night. Fortunately, the gates weighed so much that the kids never got very far with them, but it was an innocent way of annoying the neighbours.

Back at my wife's home, her father Luke would hold a small party for the neighbour kids. In front of the glowing fire he would tell the ancient stories of the Banshee and how its screeching wail would foretell of a coming death to those that heard it. Invariably, the kids would be scared to death. Having finally recovered, they would play games, simple affairs such as an Apple Dunk in which the participants were certain to get a drowning as they searched in vain for the apples that floated in the metal basin of water.

Then the lads and lasses would receive treats that might include packets of potato chips and fizzy drinks. And finally, they would cut the Hallowe'en Brack, a dense fruitcake made of flour, nuts and assorted dried and candied fruit. Within the cake a golden ring lay in waiting. He or she who received the ring with their serving of Brack would be sure to marry the next year (unlikely, of course, in that the tiny revellers were all only mere youngsters).

With the cakes and drinks taken the kids would venture to the bonfire, watching as the older kids (with the help of adults) lit it. The fire would light up the huge pile of tinder-stuff, and within moments the world seemed to come alive in a mountainous conflagration, certain to frighten away even the most remorseless of devils.

Today Hallowe'en is celebrated much as it is in the States, though with certain twists that are truly Irish. The kids dress up as savages and ghouls and walk from door to door in search of sweets. They even screech 'Trick or Treat' when knocking boldly on the door.

But the young ghouls also manage to transport legal (and illegal) fireworks down into the Republic from their Northern Irish brethren who can purchase these legally. For hours (and even days beforehand) the Irish countryside comes alive with blossoming fiery displays of rockets and the boom of large explosives.

But despite the modernisation of the holiday, we still have the bonfire and the occasional ghost story. And on a dark Hallowe'en night you can still venture into the Cemetery where you can listen for the call of the Banshee, the ancient ghost of a woman who brushes her hair as she wails her call of doom, and the screech that is certain to mark a quick and uncomfortable passing for those that hear her.

But should you try it know that you'll be venturing out on your own. Banshees are real. I know. My father-in-law told me so because he heard the wail of the Banshee and two days later a neighbour dropped dead.

Saint Patrick's Day

When coming here I had thought that St Patrick's Day just had to be *the* day of celebration on the Irish calendar. After all, as the patron saint of Ireland, St Patrick was bound to be a cause for a long and enjoyable bit of craic throughout the country. Having celebrated St Patrick's Day as I had in many American towns and cities in the U.S. (including Chicago, New York, and San Francisco) I had been under the impression that the occasion would be celebrated with much more hoopla in Ireland.

Like many other things about this country I soon discovered that I was wrong.

While the Irish celebrate St Patrick's Day in a certain Irish style, it is very unlike the celebrations of their American cousins. In fact, the Irish look at the American methods of enjoying that holiday with considerable bemusement. An American St Patrick's Day includes ornate parades and enough green to paint a mile wide line between New York and the Moon. As you possibly know, everything seems to be green on the U.S. version of the day in question: green beer, green bagels, and rivers painted a peculiar shade of green. The Irish can only giggle at America's over-wrought efforts.

In Ireland, St Patrick's Day is a much more reserved affair. As a national holiday everyone has the day off, which is a good thing in that it allows many more people to run to the local pub. But the Irish would never put a green tinge in their beer: that would be a sin and a waste of a pleasurable pint. Nor do they paint their rivers green, nor fill their bellies with green bagels; they do not hang signs that say 'Kiss me, I'm Irish!' nor do they adorn their homes with green outdoor lights.

Instead, the Irish celebrate in a much more homely fashion. First, they troop to the stores, there purchasing live green shamrock which they plant firmly in the nearest buttonhole. Many put bacon and cabbage on the boil, the cooking process of which fills their homes with the scent of salt and vinegar.

In that Saint Patrick's Day occurs during the season of Lent, and because many Irish give up the drink for forty days during that period, the Day is also a time of leniency because many will cast off their abstinence and head to the local establishment for a few well-deserved pints of black if only for the day. 'Drowning the Shamrock' on St Pat's Day is a national institution, and one that can be enjoyed by anyone old enough – or brazen enough – to sidle up to their local bar.

If you live in a larger village or town as we do, the next stop is the local parade. On this day hundreds of such parades take place all over the country. In Navan, the St Patrick's Day parade committee will consider just about anything to add to the parade and hence make it more colourful. Therefore, you might spend an hour in the damp cold of March 17th watching as what seems to be the entire county marches down the main road. There will be the Ceili band from Athboy, the Pipers from Kells, the accordion players from Kentstown, almost all of them dressed in green, orange and white. Local clubs, holding their broad and colourful banners high, will step proudly down the street as neighbours call out in welcome or with catcalls, depending on their predisposition.

Clowns might come next, throwing sweets to the children that nestle protectively between their parents. Farm tractors follow, each towing a small float created by local schools or businesses, their owners perched precariously on their uneven surfaces, freezing in the damp.

This mad spectacle will wind its way around the town, finally ending up in the village square. There, a forty-foot flatbed trailer will have been decked out in the green and gold of Ireland. On it, a Ceili band – an assortment of pipers and fiddlers – will play madly as dancers slap the floor in imitation of the much larger Riverdance.

The pubs, now well opened, will be serving pints and small ones of Irish whiskey to beat the band. Locals will wander out clutching their large glasses, bravely pushing away the cold by wearing thick anoraks and topcoats.

When the parade is finished we'll all troop home, there to enjoy the meal of bacon, cabbage and spuds. If we can fit it in there might be a small slice of apple tart and cream together with a cup of tea. After that perhaps we'll all march back down to the pub to finish off the day in a particularly Irish manner: drinking a pint while listening to a small group of fiddlers play rebel songs, their voices reaching to the sky.

Saint Patrick's Day is the national holiday. Yet it also represents something else: the coming of Christianity to this country. And though we Irish can seem to forget it, we recognise that Patrick in many ways defines this small island. It was he, after all, who helped to bring the light of hope into Ireland. And despite our somewhat drunken revelry, that coming of the light is still remembered.

On the Hill of Slane, only a few miles distant from my home, a group of people will light the Pascal fire, a small bonfire within which burns the Irish hope for a future of goodness. Hundreds of years ago a similar fire was lit, purportedly by Patrick himself. On his Day we replicate that simple gesture, acknowledging the freedom that this country now enjoys after so many years of servitude.

And the Summer Holidays

If you decide to live in this country one of the first things that you'll discover is the fact that the Irish – as well as most Europeans – have something in vast quantities that Americans and many other nationalities can only envy. And that something is holiday time.

In Ireland employers are legally obligated to give their employees almost a month of paid holiday leave. If you work hard to properly string these days of freedom together, you will not only be able to take a considerable amount of time off over the Christmas period, but will also be able to manage two whole weeks off over the summer. And the joy of it all!

As already mentioned, the Irish winters are often an impossibly horrid period of dark nights when we all believe that the sun has deserted us forever. However, as the winter turns to spring and then to summer, the sun reverses itself. Sun up is so early that it surprises even the earliest of early birds. Twilight can last almost to midnight. It's wonderful!

During the summer the Irish make certain that they enjoy themselves by taking advantage of the incredibly long days and that two weeks of liberty. In that the country is located so far to the north (look on a map – Irish latitudes are as far north as Canada's

Hudson Bay), summers can be rather chilly compared to similar periods in, say, Chicago, Berlin, Florida, London, or New York. A good day, with the clouds driven away by a summer sun, can get up to the mid-70's (low 20's Centigrade). While we have even warmer days, with highs of eighty degrees Fahrenheit and more (high-20's C), those periods are positively unusual and the Irish almost die in the poxy heat.

But when the sun is out, and though it might be cooler, the days feel warmer than what might be reflected on any thermometer, undoubtedly due to the high latitudes that we enjoy. Again, there is something magical about a proper Irish summer. Not that we have them every year, mind you. Many is the summer that we've all stood looking up at a dark blanket of cloud, temperatures in the low 50's (10 degrees C), the streets awash with a cold pouring rain, and wonder what the hell happened. Occasionally, summer will entirely forget to come to Ireland and we'll all go nuts thinking that now we'll have to wait for a whole year to see the sun, while also knowing that our Vitamin C intake will have to be increased in order to avoid scurvy.

But despite the occasional disastrous years, we have our wonderful summers, too. And during those periods you won't have to go anywhere else in the world to enjoy yourself.

Being social animals, the Irish love to get together in vast flocks that don't have to work very hard to enjoy each other's company. The beaches are awash in people. Kids throw themselves into the cold Irish Sea on the east coast, or the even colder Atlantic on the west coast, hoping to create an Irish version of *Bay Watch*. While they do this, their parents plant large screens of fabric on the beach in hopes of keeping away the chilly Irish breeze. Behind these thin bulwarks, they search desperately for a tan with which to impress partners and friends, invariably burning their unprotected skin to cinders in the process.

If not the beach, the Irish will venture to any number of festivals and gatherings held throughout the country. Fleah's, an Irish celebration of dance and music, and Country Fairs will be held in many towns and villages countrywide. At these affairs the populace gathers for singsong, many pints, and great craic as they enjoy the music and dance of their ancestors. Ploughing competitions, celebrating the nation's agrarian roots, will be mounted on fields throughout the country. There you can watch tractor go head to head with tractor, or see ancient steam threshers at work, or learn how farmers used the wide blade of a scythe in the old days with which they broke their backs in cutting the acres of hay from their stony fields.

If you'd rather avoid the crowds then visit the old castle that will invariably reside just down the road and spend some time sitting in the warming grass, perhaps breaking out a fulfilling lunch of sandwiches and flasks of tea. Or if you'd rather get some exercise, then put on your hiking boots and take off for long walks upon Ireland's miles of hiking trails. It being the summer, you're bound to run into hundreds of foreign tourists who are also enjoying the natural beauty of Ireland and you'll have the guilty pleasure of knowing that they would envy your position if they knew that you had thrown caution to the winds and had emigrated to this country, and are now free to take the pleasure of the Irish countryside whenever you choose to do so.

But the Irish aren't content to spend their summers only in their home country. In the hunt for guaranteed sunshine they now search the world for new corners to enjoy. And why wouldn't they when the rest of Europe beckons, and with foreign holiday prices and airfares now so low? With the coming of new competition in the airline and travel industries, the Irish have hundreds of summer destinations to choose from.

For years, Spain was by far the favourite. Back when I came here, and with the national economy in the gutter, an Irish person who was fortunate enough to visit Torremolinos for a week was considered to have found heaven. But now such a place is considered something of a dive. Instead, the Irish pack their bags and head to the four corners of the globe: in Europe favourites include Portugal, Greece, France, Turkey and the Cannery Islands. Moving farther a-field, Thailand and Vietnam are now visited more frequently by the Irish. Going in the other direction, and due to the relative strength of the euro against the U.S. dollar, Florida and much of the Americas – including Cuba – are now firm favourites.

But wherever they go the Irish bring with them their joy of life and uniquely Irish sense of conviviality. They'll be the first up to the bar, the first on the dance floors, the first to be cajoled into taking part in a ridiculous stunt by a floorshow host, the first to start a conversation, and the first to break out in belly laughs full of living. For you see, the Irish enjoy themselves so much because they really do their best not to take life too seriously. And when on holidays, the Irish can't seem to take life seriously at all.

The Irish enjoy their summer holidays just as much as they enjoy Christmas, Hallowe'en, St Patrick's Day, and all of the other days in between. They do their best to embrace these precious days of freedom, experiencing each new person, each new place, each new activity, to its very fullest. The rest of the world might be puzzled at the antics of the Irish but the Irish don't seem to mind a bit. After all, they've discovered a secret: they've learned how to enjoy the greatest gift that we've all been given.

Life itself.

Guideline Twelve
Toward an Understanding of Ireland's Sporting Mania

Upon being asked why his team was so successful in the 1990 World Cup, an unidentified Irish Football fan replied:

'Like it's pretty straightforward, like. The team was great, the manager was great, and as for the fans? Fucking brilliant!'

I must admit that I am not the greatest sports fan in the world. This predisposition probably goes back to those heady days of my childhood: at a mere ten years of age, and believing as every other kid on my block did that I was certain to be the next Mickey Mantle (a Superman of a baseball player in case you didn't know), I tried out for the local Little League Baseball Team. With a pop fly hit in my direction, and knowing that my actions were certainly being scrutinised by a cadre of adult coaches and sneering, weasel-like school chums, I backed up … up … up … reaching for the ball, never taking my eyes from it…and promptly fell on my ass. With the laughter of coaches and other ten-year-olds ringing in my ears I fled the field, deciding then and there that sports of any description just weren't my thing.

But despite my lack of interest in the sporting world, no book on Ireland can be complete without a chapter devoted specifically to sports. For you see the Irish are mad about sports. And they have so many to choose from! Gaelic sports, football, horseracing, rugby, polo, billiards and snooker – the list seems endless.

If you decide to become one with the Irish, and no matter what your own predisposition regarding sports, you will undoubtedly be sucked into this exciting madness just like I was.

When I first moved to Ireland I admitted to a complete ignorance of the local games. I had a hard enough time understanding the basics of American sports. Baseball, American football, basketball and ice hockey were the sum total of my sporting universe – and I had enough trouble struggling with those. Consequently, and when my wife and I would wander into the local pub for a well-deserved drink, I had a difficult time talking with the local natives and in particular the males of that species in that all they seemed to do was converse about the matches, players, and scores of the teams that had beaten each other senseless only the day before.

For the longest time I would take my drink alone, thinking that I would never fit in simply because I had no interest in what my Irish cousins were so very focused upon.

All of that changed in 1990.

If you are an American reading this, you possibly understand that soccer is the world's most popular sport. Known as 'football' in this part of the world – and the rest of the world as a matter of fact – and not to be confused with the American variety, billions of people passionately follow the 'beautiful game', as it has become known across the globe. Nowhere is this truer than in Ireland.

Football in Ireland is played at a variety of amateur, semi-professional, and professional levels. But while the Irish might follow some of their local teams, their real passion is focused upon English teams. I still can't figure this out. Though the Irish are supposed to espouse a negative view of the English due to history, and though they may seem to desire to punch the English senseless whenever the Irish National Football Team happens to share a football pitch with an English National Football Team, never ask an Irishman or woman to betray their loyalty to English soccer. Many follow Manchester United, Liverpool, Arsenal and a host of other English football clubs as if their lives depended on it.

The International Football season changes all that, of course. In Europe and the rest of the world – even in the United States – each nation fields its own national soccer team. Every four years those teams pit their skills and national honour against each other as they vie for the World Cup, one of Sporting's most prestigious championships. If you are European or from most other countries in the world, you will instantly understand the passion and general craziness that surrounds this series of matches. If, on the other hand, you are from North America you possibly won't understand why what seems to be the entire world becomes so obsessed during the World Cup season. If you are one of those unfortunates, and should you decide to reside in Ireland or most anywhere else in the world, you'd best become educated.

For many years, the Irish didn't have very much to get excited about when it came to the World Cup Championship. The Irish national football team, those erstwhile Irish players assembled from other national squads to play for the World Cup, had never achieved very much. Then in 1988 and 1989 Irish soccer fans noticed a difference. A new manager had taken over. An English fellow as it turned out; a tall man who wore a soft cap and carried a loud voice, and who knew exactly how he wanted his team to play. And the Irish team started to win. Suddenly, the locals had something to natter about.

Having no interest in sports I didn't notice much, of course. But in 1990, as the World Cup approached and with my parents once again in town on a visit, my goodly wife suggested that we all troop down to the local pub to watch what at that point were the beginnings of the 1990 World Cup play-offs. As it turned out, the Irish team was in the thick of it.

'You mean you want to spend an entire evening watching soccer?' I had croaked. 'It sounds so boring! What about my father? He'll fall asleep!'

'It's called football over here,' she had replied, not taking no for an answer. 'Stop snivelling. You'll all love it.' And so I packed up my parents, put on a bright green wholly hat that my wife insisted that I wear, and headed down to our local drinking establishment, knowing that we were facing into an evening of certain boredom.

The pub was packed. And I don't mean just crowded. I mean *packed*. When the four of us squeezed into the standing room only crowd you couldn't have put a toothpick between us. 'What the hell is going on?' my father wanted to know. 'Shut up, mate,' the fellow next to us stated reverently. 'Charlton is taking the field.'

We looked up at the giant television screen that had been bolted to the wall for this special occasion, watching as the Irish manager took the field, followed by his team of seasoned players. In the pub, the sea of Irishmen and women peered anxiously toward the television's flickering screen as if watching the Second Coming. 'Who's playing?' I asked my wife.

'Where have you been?' the guy next to us stated. 'It's Ireland versus England. If we beat them – if we even tie them – we're off to Italy and the finals!'

The game – called a match over here – started. I knew that I was going to be bored to death. What I hadn't counted on was the emotion that the Irish fans would display. As the game moved along, and when England scored one over on the Irish, the entire pub descended into a pit of despair. I turned to my father, noting the glazed look on his face, thinking that maybe it was time to go home.

'We're not going anywhere,' my wife hissed.

And so we waited. The eyes of the Irish fans were all locked onto the television. The ball moved downfield. The packed pub sensed an opportunity. On the TV screen the Irish forward swung back a large boot, kicked with all of his might, and the ball rocketed into the English net.

The pub exploded in delight. Honestly, you would have thought that the roof of that small building would have come off. The Irish fans roared their pleasure like a pride of victorious lions. The decibels that they generated would seem to have broken glass. They jumped up and down. They pounded each other's backs. They poured beer over each other. Obviously, a sporting miracle had taken place.

This same scene of revelry was replicated in small towns, larger villages, and entire cities over the width and breadth of Ireland as the entire country came unglued. Even today, fifteen years later, the Irish talk about that match and that single goal with hushed voices approaching reverence.

I had never heard or seen anything like the uproar that took place that night. Not at any game that I had ever attended, anywhere. I was hooked. Ireland was in the 1990 World Cup, and finally – after eight years of living in that wonderful country – I finally began to understand just how important sports were to that populace.

The Irish people take their sports very seriously. Many Irish people follow their chosen brand of sport like a religion. When a national team plays, the country's fans bleed green and orange. Legions of Irish men and women will travel the globe to support their teams.

During that World Cup for instance, many Irish took out second mortgages or otherwise incurred substantial debt in order to parade around the world in support of the national football team. Those Irish who couldn't afford to travel took special delight in literally closing down the country as they headed toward their local pub in order to watch the various matches as Ireland clawed through the competition. During those games, the roads were deserted. The country had come to a standstill as Irish fans everywhere watched their team play against stiff competition.

The Irish have been a sporting nation since time immemorial. Their official national sports – Gaelic football and Gaelic hurling – are mentioned in Irish folklore. Both of these sports illustrate the competitive, yet crazed, nature of the Irish.

To this American, Gaelic football seems rather like a combination of soccer, rugby, and American football. Fifteen insanely strong and athletic players on each team (or 'side' as a team is called in this part of the world) attempt to get their hands, feet, or body around a round ball. The objective of the game is to either score by kicking the ball through an upright at the end of the field (or 'pitch' as the playing field is known over here) for a single point, or by putting the ball into a net that rests underneath the upright for three points.

Like soccer, the game is non-stop. Players must 'dribble' the ball, meaning that they can only hold it for three steps. Otherwise they must kick it, bat it, or somehow attempt to throw it to another team member. Each county in Ireland has their own Gaelic football team. The players are 'non-professional', meaning that they don't receive any pay. Yet their commitment and professionalism is unquestioned as they attempt to bring honour to their county by winning the All-Ireland Championship.

My hometown of Navan resides in County Meath. The county, for all intent and purposes, is Gaelic football mad. Come the GAA season, the county's folk troop down to the local County Football Pitch to watch the Meath Team as it attempts to beat other county teams senseless, and thereby win the match. Over the years, the Meath players have done a fairly good job at this. Not only have the managed to destroy their opponents upon numerous occasions, but in the years since I've taken up residency here, have also managed to win the All-Ireland Championship any number of times. Upon those occasions the town of Navan has literally gone crazy as the victorious Meath players march through its small streets and the roar of drunken revelry is raised in joyous approval.

This celebration of victory must certainly hark back to times thousands of years ago when the Kings of Tara, based only a few miles from modern Navan, would march home from their wars to the acclaim of their fellow Irishmen and women. I suspect that Irish Football is simply a reflection of those days long ago, and gives the Irish something to cheer about without the need to resort to conflict of the bloody kind.

But if Gaelic Football is crazed, its sister sport – Gaelic Hurling – is insane. In my humble opinion, this is a madman's game. Like Gaelic Football it is a game played between fifteen players on each side. Again, the objective is to get a ball either over an upright for one point, or into a net for three points. But there the similarity ends.

Hurling is one of the fastest, wildest – and possibly most dangerous – games in the world. It originated in Ireland before the days of Christianity. The earliest written reference to Hurling is contained in the Brehon Laws of the fifth century A.D. While I've never read the Brehon Laws, I'm certain that it must contain a list of casualties that were suffered by local players as they attempted to hack through the opposition.

For you see in this game of wondrous skill, each player is armed with an incredibly strong ash stick, seemingly as deadly as a steel girder, known as a hurly. Approximately three feet long, and with a flat surface carved at one end, players use this stick to move a small, hard ball called a zlither downfield in hopes of scoring a goal.

These fellows run pell-mell down the pitch, keeping an eye out for the uprights at the end of the field, all the while balancing the small ball at the end of the hurly. In a flat run, and approaching the goal, hurling players will then toss the ball straight up while pulling their sticks back, finally smashing the zlither toward the far goalposts in a mighty blow.

Should an opposing team member's head, arm, or back happen to get in the way of that strong ash stick so much the better. Heads, arms, legs, and assorted body parts might litter the field after a match but that's just part of the adventure. Unlike American football where players wear padding that protects them much like armoured knights of days gone by, hurling players wear very little, if anything, to offer them protection from the shattering might of a hurly stick.

But the Irish penchant for sport does not stop at soccer or Gaelic games. The Irish also field winning professional rugby teams. Only last year, the Irish Rugby Team won International Rugby's Triple Crown. The Irish have also participated successfully in the Olympics, winning Gold, Silver, and Bronze medals in horse jumping, swimming, and track.

The Irish also follow horse racing, many doing so as if their lives depended on it. Betting shops – or Turf Accountants, as they are called over here – are often crowded as the Irish put their hard-earned money down on the warm nose of their choice, watching the flickering television as they determine whether they have won or lost a fortune.

Ireland is sports mad. When their teams are playing the entire country might come to a stop as the locals determine whether or not their favourite teams are winning or losing. If they are winning, you can be certain that much of the country will be crowded into the local pubs in order to watch the excitement. If they are losing, you can be sure that many Irish will be gathered in the pub anyway, if only to commiserate over a tall, cold pint.

While you can survive in this country even if you do not particularly enjoy soccer, rugby or hurling, it does help if you know enough to be able to hold up your end of a sporting conversation down at the local. Otherwise, you may end up sitting in a dark corner, forlorn and forgotten.

But if you can learn enough about sports to roar madly at the local teams like the Irish do, you'll find life here much more enjoyable. Do that and Irish will surely embrace you as one of their own.

Guideline Thirteen
Living & Dying the Irish Way

Overheard at a local country wake as the recently departed was being viewed:
'Ah, now doesn't he look like himself? And he really did know how to live didn't he? Now let's get out of here and grab a pint before he wakes up and spoils the day on us.'

When I first came to this country I decided to take a tour of our small town and spent a day walking through its narrow streets and byways. The roadways were deserted because of the light rain that fell and having taken a look at the small variety of newsagents, chemists, picture houses, green grocers, coal merchants, and drapers in which I could spend my non-existent cash, I suddenly felt a certain parching of the throat and knew that it was time to get out of the rain and grab a pint.

In that Navan had over thirty pubs to choose from I knew that a pint would soon be resting at my elbow. Looking across the small main street I spied Fitzers's Pub, a well-known local watering hole, and made a mad dash across the potholed surface of the road, entering the establishment where I hoped to find warmth and company.

The pub was packed but the good-natured locals made room for me as I sidled up to the bar. 'Pint of black,' I said, shaking the rain from my jacket.

'Soft day,' the barkeep observed.

'Is it?' I stated shortly, feeling the cold fingers of rain run down my neck. I watched as he filled the pint, then put it aside to rest.

As I waited my eyes adjusted to the dark warmth of the bar. And as they did I noticed a curious thing. The bar was roughly split into three sections. In the middle section the owner kept his supplies of beverage, enough to sink a ship: taps that poured what seemed to be endless quantities of Guinness, Smithwick's Ale, and Harp Lager rose from behind the counter like a small forest of

175

stainless steel; large bottles of spirits were bolted to the wall, resting vertically, draining into the small optics that held exact measures of fiery whiskies, ports, gins, and vodkas. Resting on shelves behind the counter were other bottles containing dark porter and mixers. But it was the other two sections that made me realise that I was living in a different world.

To the right of the dark mahogany wood of the bar was a section devoted entirely to foodstuffs: tins of baked beans, spaghetti hoops, soups, pots of mustard and the like rested on narrow shelves that completely covered one wall, rising, it seemed, into the dark recesses of the high ceiling. A whole cooked ham and a block of cheese sat regally behind a glass case. Loaves of sliced bread filled a wide shelf. One of them had been opened, sitting on a block of wood, breadcrumbs and bits of ham and cheese covering the counter. Obviously, the barkeep's customers had recently taken their lunch here.

But it was the third section of the bar that really got my attention, though what I saw seemed so entirely out of context with the rest of the establishment that I had trouble believing what my eyes were certainly communicating to my rain-soaked brain.

Memorial wreaths of every description covered one wall. Plastic flowers of reds, pastels, whites, and mauves, wrapped in tight ovals, hung like grim sentinels above me. Wine coloured ribbons overprinted with white epithets bearing remarks such as "In Deepest Sympathy", were tied reverently to the wreaths, seeming to whisper their grim intentions.

Just below the display of wreaths I noticed a small but carefully painted sign:

Padraig Fitzer, Undertaker
Funerals and Memorials Available

I quickly picked up my pint and took a deep drink.

'Ya' all right?' the barkeep asked, having noticed my disbelieving look.

I pointed to the contents on his wall with a somewhat unsteady hand. The barkeep smiled broadly, reached over and patted me on the shoulder. 'Ah, it's the Irish way,' he stated. 'Don't you know, you can drink, eat and die in this place.'

While such an all-in-one facility might well be available in the United States I have never seen one. For all I know, Wal-Mart might be thinking of such a strategy in order to further increase its market share, though I doubt it.

But no matter what is happening in the U.S., and upon further reflection, the Irish ability to develop an establishment that allows a person such an all-encompassing facility all under the one roof seems entirely appropriate and is indicative of the Irish attitude to life. For you see, the Irish not only know how to live but also have developed an uncanny ability to accept the inevitability of death. And they celebrate the lives of those who have died in a way that at first seemed entirely foreign to me but which now seems entirely appropriate and sensible.

Death, of course, is inevitable and unless an archaeologist manages to locate the Fountain of Youth or a geneticist finally discovers a method to manipulate our genes, a visit by the Grim Reaper will always be humanity's final outcome. In the U.S., however, the inevitability of this certain outcome is not taken lightly. Americans will do almost anything to postpone this final curtain: they will try to halt the aging process with help from the latest dietary fad; they'll spend vast fortunes on unguents and lotions that promise to delay the day of aging; they'll struggle with exercise regimes that could kill even the strongest of them. No matter what they do, of course, death is always around the final corner, waiting to take its due. But until that grim day, many Americans seem to do what they can to push the grisly thoughts of the inevitable from their minds.

The Irish, on the other hand, seem to recognise that Death is a part of living. While it is not exactly embraced (who in their right minds wants to die?), it is recognised as being an unavoidable part of the circle of life.

And this results in some unique and very human customs.

Saying Goodbye

I've never been to a first-class wake, even after all my years of living here. Wakes, as they used to be performed, seem to have gone out of fashion in Ireland though I've heard of them still happening in the West of the country. Apparently, wakes are something to behold.

A Survivor's Guide to Living in Ireland

On the day of death, the surviving family members will drape all of the mirrors of the house in simple cloth and open the doors and windows of the home in order to provide the soul of the dead with an easy departure. With his or her soul now on the way to Heaven family members will also quickly gather the material possessions of the departed, distributing them to relatives, friends, or charities. In this way, the soul has nothing to beckon them back from their Heavenly journey.

Now the wake begins in earnest. As I understand it, a wake not only allows friends and relatives a chance to say goodbye to the departed and pay their respects to the surviving family but also provides a great excuse for a few days of uproarious living.

The dear departed, dressed in their best and laid out in the simple mahogany casket, will have been delivered to the family home the day following their death. Usually laid out in the family living room and surrounded by all that they knew and loved, the entire village might turn out to pay their last respects.

These people will form a huge line, passing through the family home, saying goodbye to the dearly departed, shaking hands with the survivor's, and saying a small prayer for everyone involved. Back in the old days, a group of hired Wailers – women who have been asked to cry and wail for the sake of the dear one's soul – would stand outside the house, creating a terrible cacophony that might rival that of the Banshee's.

As part of the wake, the local publican might have delivered a huge supply of porter and whiskey, and the locals will stand in the garden drinking themselves toward oblivion as they recount tremendous stories of the person who has passed away. Sometimes, and depending on the status of the departed, a successful wake could last for days.

In most of today's Ireland, wakes are a thing of the past. That said the Irish still manage to honour their dead in a manner that also allows them to embrace the glory of living. Possibly the most celebratory funeral I was fortunate enough to attend was that of Jenny (which is not her real name), a close friend of mine. She died young, at the age of only fifty-two. Her funeral was held in her mother's home, a simple structure located only a few doors down from my wife's parent's house.

Jenny died of cancer. For a few weeks prior to the end she was confined to hospital. But in the last few days she was permitted to go home. Because we all knew that she had only days left, we spent a great deal of time visiting with her. Jenny wasn't too worried about what the future would hold. Instead, she revelled in the company of her family and friends. Each of us, in our individual ways, said goodbye. And finally, succumbing to the inevitable, she left us.

Jenny's death occurred during the Christmas season. She was lovingly dressed in a new tracksuit that her husband gave to her and placed in a beautiful mahogany casket which rested in her parent's living room. Because the house was small, all of her friends gathered in the freezing December weather at the front of her home. We formed a small queue and by turns entered the house to bid our final goodbyes.

Many of us took Jenny's hand to say farewell. We each sprinkled holy water on her head. Then we stepped back out into the night. I will never forget that night; the frosty cold of the Christmas evening and the clear bells of the local church as they tolled a clarion of Silent Night. When all of us had paid our last respects, the casket was closed and brought from the house. We then formed a funeral cortege, walking behind the hearse that held Jenny's remains to St Mary's Church, located just down the road.

There, the local priest helped us to say our goodbye's within the dimly lit yet Christmas bright confines of the Church. And when he had finished we again formed a queue, each of us shaking the hands of Jenny's relatives, letting them know of our love for this woman and the fact that she had helped us experience life a little more fully.

The next day Jenny was buried in a simple ceremony. Again, those that loved her walked behind the hearse as it made its way up to the cemetery. At the graveside, we all said one last farewell. Finally, Jenny was laid to rest.

Later that day some of us gathered in a local hotel, there to have a drink and a sandwich, laughing at the memory of this remarkable person, recounting the many joys that she had brought to us all. It was a gathering that not only cherished and celebrated Jenny's life, but that also celebrated our own. When we had finished we walked out of the hotel determined to make the most of the days that we each had left on this planet.

Dying is inevitable. But somehow the Irish have learned to make it a part of living. To that end, they also have figured out a way to make it not quite as frightening.

A Walk with Past Friends

On any given Sunday afternoon, when we have nothing else to do, my goodly wife might look across the living room at me, toward the lump snoring from behind the Sunday papers, and ask: 'Want to go up to the cemetery?' And rather than say, 'What, are you out of your mind?' I'll reply instead, 'Sure, why not?'

We'll throw a rake into the back of the car, perhaps bring the dog, and motor off the mile or two to the local repository for the dead of Navan.

In many places throughout Ireland cemeteries are treated somewhat like public parks. On a sunny day you'll find these places crowded as people tend to the graves of their loved ones, enjoy a chin-wag or two with living friends or neighbours, take a walk to see who has recently met their Maker, or simply enjoy the day.

When I first arrived in Ireland I thought this to be a rather macabre custom. After all, I had never before taken a trip to a cemetery with the intention of simply visiting the place unless it was of some historical importance. Visiting the graveyard in Ireland is different. It offers a chance to take some much-needed time out. At the same time, it allows all of us to confront and accept the inevitable.

For instance when Kathleen, my mother-in-law, was still alive we would regularly drive up to the cemetery with her in order to visit the grave of her late husband and there to weed the plot and visit with whomever happened to be around. In that Luke, my late father-in-law, happened to be interred in the family grave and in that wives are invariably buried beside their husbands, Kathleen recognised that someday she too would be residing next to him. Yet her reaction to the inevitable was not a cause for tears but rather for jokes:

Me: 'Are you sad when you visit, Nana (we always called Kathleen "Nana")?'

Her: 'Not at all. One day you can plant me right here. I'll be pushing up the daisies. And if it's full, just put me in the back garden. I'll do just fine there.'

I'd smile uncertainly, then she'd laugh gaily and we'd all get back to pulling weeds from the small gravesite.

Kathleen passed away a couple of years ago, at the relatively young age of seventy-five. We buried her next to her husband, Bernie's father, and we do our best to visit them both a couple of times a year. I know now that visits of this type help all of us not only to accept what has happened to our loved ones, but to also realise that this final inevitability will also happen to ourselves.

And in doing so, many also gain a certain acceptance that perhaps death – as a part of living – isn't so bad after all. Not if you can rest in a pretty park, with a huge variety of marble and stone monuments surrounding you, listening to your friends and neighbours as they walk over to say hello and pull a weed or two.

Guideline Fourteen
When You Come Here You Might Never Leave

Navan, County Meath   *September 11, 2001*

Dear Mom and Dad,

Are you both okay? I couldn't believe what I saw. We rang Junior. He had been driving along the 57th Street Bridge when it happened and saw one of the towers collapse. He thought it was Armageddon. Thank God he came out of it all right.

I can't believe it nor can anyone else. I just wish I was home right now. Today, more than any other day, I know that while I've made my home here I am still an American. And rightly proud I am of it.

The Irish have been wonderful. You wouldn't believe the outpouring of sympathy. While I would rather be with you, at least I know just how much these people care for us. Everyone seems to be praying. Their prayers have helped me enormously to cope with the unthinkable.

I'll write again later and phone you this evening if I can get through. I love you,

Tom

The trouble with Ireland is simple. If you come here, you might never ever find the strength to leave no matter if you suffer from misfortune or experience an incredible stroke of luck. You might moan about the place. You might find yourself to be intolerably homesick. You might even find perfectly logical reasons to journey back to your homeland: the distance from relatives, the prospects of an incredible job and career move, or the simple emotions of wanting to go home.

Move here and the odds are that you'll never go back. But though you may stay, you will undoubtedly be torn apart by uncertainty, wondering if you've made the right decision; often wracked by a sense of loss and despair that perhaps your decision has been the wrong one and that you should move back. But then you'll put off the decision and stay another day, and then another. But as the days pass, you'll still hear a confused voice in your inner ear once again saying: 'Am I really doing the right thing?'

I offer this warning because it's something to think about before you choose the path of immigration, and the emotional plight of an immigrant is an issue that I find is rarely discussed. Immigrating is hard work. It can be an emotional roller coaster out of which few emerge unscathed. But something magical happens when a person moves here. Despite all of the difficulties of immigrating to this country that I have previously mentioned, Ireland seems to root itself into the very fabric of your being. And once the roots have become established it's very difficult to shake yourself loose.

Let me tell you two stories: one a riddle, the other a story from my own experience, that might explain this point.

The riddle goes like this: a friend of mine, an Australian immigrant, recently asked me to name the second most miserable person in the world. I guessed and guessed and couldn't come up with an answer. It turns out that the second most miserable person in the world is an expatriate.

Then he asked me to name the most miserable person in the world. Again I couldn't come up with the answer. It turns out that the most miserable person in the world is an expatriate who has returned home.

Departing on the adventure of immigration is not to be taken lightly. For years I second-guessed my decision, thinking that I would be much happier and much more successful if I had stayed in the States. When in the dark throes of homesickness I would look to the West and think that the grass beyond the horizon had to be much greener than the Irish variety that I found growing beneath my naked feet. At times I believed that I was going to go crazy with the thoughts of my homeland.

And on occasion I'd return home on a holiday and during my stay seriously think that perhaps I should really consider a move back to the U.S.

But there's a problem. I've changed. I am no longer just an American. Because of the length of my stay here I am also Irish and hence also a European. And I find that I've come to think with a somewhat European view of things. This means that I am no longer entirely comfortable with the U.S. And I realise that if I went home I would in all probability find it as difficult to fit in there as I did when arriving in Ireland.

It's a sad state of affairs because I've always loved my homeland. But I realise now that perhaps I can never go home.

Ireland has captured my heart. I've already written about many of the aspects of Irish life that have caused this. But if you come here you'll understand that which I often have so much difficulty in putting into words.

For this reason, perhaps this next story will illustrate that which I can't adequately describe. The start of this story occurred on what is a dark day in the world's history, and certainly what must be the darkest day in American history. It starts on September 11, 2001.

That day I had a meeting in Dublin with a business client. I was sitting in a boardroom when one of the client's secretaries came in. She announced to all of us that an attack had occurred in New York.

Knowing that I was American my clients – who have now become close friends – were more than a little concerned for me and mine. Rather than just expressing concern and continuing with the meeting they reached out with their minds and hearts and supported me because they knew instinctively how upset I had become.

They walked me out of the conference room to a television that was tuned to CNN. I arrived just in time to see the collapse of the second World Trade Centre tower.

Like many Americans throughout the world, I too collapsed. The client's marketing manager held me in his arms as I cried and cried. And you know what? He never made me feel in the least embarrassed. Instead, he let me know that it was perfectly okay for me to be a human being as, on that terrible day, I cried for my fellow citizens.

When I finally got home on that dreadful evening I found my house to be awash with neighbours who had come to express their concern. Their eyes were also filled with tears. They were stunned by the uncontrollable events that had engulfed us.

They offered to me, a person who in their eyes represented the people of the United States, their sympathy, their support and their prayers.

Two days later, the Taoiseach – the Prime Minister of the Irish government – decided that the events that had taken place in the United States required an appropriate response. For hundreds of years America has held a special place in the hearts of the Irish. For that reason, the Taoiseach determined that the best way that the nation could possibly express its sympathy was to close the country down in a Day of Mourning, a day that would demonstrate to the world the extent of Irish grief and solidarity.

And that's precisely what he did. To my knowledge, Ireland is the only country in the world that marked this desperately sad occasion with a National Day of Mourning.

That night what seemed to be every person in the country flocked to their local church. My wife and I went to St Mary's Church in Navan with our children. I've never seen so many people there, not even at Christmas. The Altar of the church was set alight with the sparkling, hopeful flames of hundreds of small candles. And in front of that bright river of glittering hope came the outpourings of sympathy from the heart of a nation, and from the hundreds of local people who expressed their own emotions of condolence so freely.

After Mass many people whom I had never had the opportunity of meeting came up to me. They had been told that I was an American who had chosen to make Ireland home both for himself and his family. Many took my elbow as they whispered words of sympathy. Others touched me gently on the chest or back in a simple gesture of kindness and comfort, and told me how very sorry they were.

I had never been as proud to be American as I was on that day. Since then it is true to say that I am also incredibly proud to be Irish.

Perhaps that is one of the reasons why I will probably never leave this country. If you come here, you will begin the journey toward an understanding of what it means to be Irish. Ireland is much more than its beautiful landscape. It is much more than its rich history or its magical ancient structures or even its people. Somehow, it is a combination of everything that has been woven together to form an attitude and joy for life that I have been unable to find elsewhere.

On that day you will not only be captivated by the experience but you will also know what it means to be truly blessed.

Guideline Fifteen
Now What? Plan, That's What!

Planning vt 1 : to arrange the parts of : DESIGN   2 : to devise or project the realisation or achievement of 3 : to have in mind : INTEND

Webster's Seventh New Collegiate Dictionary

So you've read the books, whipped through the tourist guides, talked it over, thought about it, spent a year of sleepless nights, and now you're determined to uproot your existence and move to Ireland. For whatever reason, perhaps because you've watched *The Quiet Man* one too many times, you've decided that your life would become much more fulfilled if you chucked everything in, sold the house, packed up your boxes, and became one with the Irish and all that their country has to offer.

What do I advise? Hold everything, that's what.

For God's sake, take it from me: don't do what I did. Prior to moving here with my good wife I had visited this country for all of two weeks. I didn't know my arse from my elbow as they say over here, and didn't have any idea of what I was getting into when I finally arrived.

I didn't understand that I was about to move to a completely different culture. And it is, you know. Perhaps because the Irish speak English with such a wonderful lilt, many people – particularly Americans – automatically believe that living here will be akin to residing in Peoria only without the benefit of a local Wal-Mart.

Ireland is different. Take my word for it. Some people love the place. Other people simply hate it. For instance, I know of one couple from Canada who moved over because the husband had been born here. His family had immigrated to Canada when he was a mere lad and he had never returned – until his ill-begotten journey.

187

Working from his home near Toronto, he landed a job with an Irish company over the Internet. Having painted a world of Irish charm to his Canadian wife, he then proceeded to sell up everything. He loaded wife and children on a plane and flew over.

A couple of weeks later a twenty-foot container holding what remained of their worldly possessions – including the family car – arrived. The family bought a house near us. They put their kids in school. They tried to settle.

As it turned out, prior to their move over his wife had never had the benefit of even a short visit. Leaving Canada, she had no idea at all that she was moving to a country whose reality was very different from the green-tinged musings of her homesick husband.

Less than two years after their arrival the wife and kids packed their bags and made their way back to Canada. The bemused husband was left behind to sell his recently purchased Irish dream home. Having finally sold he left without a whimper.

I've never seen them since. I worry that they are now divorced and that he is living in a squalid pond populated by bellowing moose as punishment for his insane judgement.

If you're considering a move to Ireland for God's sake be careful. Think about it. Do some research. Then take some time out and visit the place. Make it a thorough visit.

Rent a car and drive through the countryside. Along the way, take the opportunity to stay at some of the best bed and breakfast's anywhere. You'll find them delightful, relatively inexpensive, and you'll have the pleasure of knowing that your Irish hostess will be taking incredible delight in parting you from your hard-earned money with the very best of intentions.

Invariably, she'll give you and your family a cup of Irish tea to make the process that much less painful.

Then climb back into your rental car. Go see the rest of place. Take a drive through big cities, small cities, larger towns, and wee villages. Get some idea of what it is that you're looking for.

Visit a few pubs and see how well you can handle your Guinness. If you're standing when everyone else has fallen you'll know that you're more than able for this country.

Find out if you can tolerate the constant rain. See if you go ballistic as the occasional pothole knocks the fillings from your teeth. Discover the outrage of high Irish taxes and prices for yourself, and see if you can not only sympathise with your Irish compatriots about the extortionate cost of living but also grin and bear it as everyone else does.

If you can do these things you might just make it here.

Then, do the other stuff. Stay away from the tourist trail and instead take a walk on a fine soft Irish day. Breath in the peat-filled air. Climb a couple of mountains. Get drunk and roar at the sheep just like some of the locals do.

Sit facing the ocean and watch as the sun sinks over the far horizon and visualise that you now live here permanently, that the next stop over that misty sea is Boston Harbour or Liverpool or Paris or wherever you're from and ask yourself how you feel about it? Would you be so homesick that you would brave anything to make the swim to the far shore and seeming civilisation? Or would you know that your home town will exist as always, only without the benefit of your presence, and that you will be incredibly happy in this small yet beautiful country.

If your answer is the latter, then you just might do it. You could uproot yourself from your present existence and settle into a culture that sparkles like a glowing, living tapestry of life.

You could survive in Ireland just as I have.

Guideline Sixteen
Learn to Talk Like the Irish.
A Dictionary of Irish Slang and Phrases

Overheard, as an English couple received a warm welcome from a local Irish tour guide:

Irishman: 'And a Cead Mile Failte to you. Yer sure to enjoy the stay, and you'll take pleasure in the back of beyonds of our country for certain or I'm a gobshite to be sure. When you go to the West, do try the poteen if you can get it down you and make certain that you have the bubble and squeak for tea.

'But stay away from Lorcan on yer travels for he's a cowboy and he'll banjax you entirely. He's only a Gossan so you shouldn't take any notice of him because he has much to learn. Now be off with you, for me throat is parched and I'm blathering on like an eejit.'

English husband to his wife: 'Audrey, what did he say?'

Both Irish and English are the official languages of this country, which means that while not all Irish understand Gaeilge (even though that is their beautiful native tongue, many Irish don't speak the traditional language at all) all of them do speak English just like you possibly do. But just because they speak English doesn't mean that you'll understand them. To survive here and really integrate into this society, you'll need to absorb the colourful English language of the Irish. Trust me, it isn't so hard and within a few months you'll be chatting, fecking and blinding just like they do.

The only problem with learning Irish slang and phrases is that they become second nature. And when you decide to go back on holidays to America or Canada, Germany or Australia – or wherever you're from – your relatives and friends will look at you as if you've gone nuts. However, it is a small price to pay knowing as you do that you live in a country far, far away and have learned to talk the talk within a culture that is decidedly different from your own.

A Survivor's Guide to Living in Ireland

If you're an American writer or have some sort of job that insists that you use the written version of the English language, all I can say is Good Luck to you. The Irish, as do the English, spell many words a little differently. You know most of them already, of course. 'Color' is 'colour'. 'Realize' and most words ending in '...ize' is 'realise'. 'Favorite' is spelled 'favourite'. But after a few months of going crazy as you attempt to remember which country you're writing for you'll soon get the hang of it. If all else fails, and you write using a Bill Gates 'Word' product, there's always Spell Check to fall back on. Just make certain that you're using the U.K. default settings.

This small dictionary will hopefully help you to navigate through some of the Irishisms that pepper the conversation of the locals. If you study it well it might help you to avoid the many difficult situations that I managed to get myself into when I first moved here. Though I heard what they said, and while I thought I understood, I discovered that I didn't understand at all!

For instance check out the Irish meaning of the word, 'Rubber', below. When I took my first job as a weighbridge salesman I had the pleasure of working with a charming and absolutely gorgeous young woman. One early morning, and without the appropriate amount of caffeine in my blood to ensure a working brain, this woman Cheryl casually asked me to lend her my Rubber.

I could swear I had heart palpitations. I began sweating. I was certain that a heart attack would follow. As my guilt-wracked mind wondered what my young wife would think of this unprovoked advance, I attempted to think of how I might answer the sweet woman who gazed at me with a face that grew more perplexed as the moment following her simple request wore on.

With my body frozen into a ridiculous posture, and with Cheryl probably believing that I was having some sort of psychotic episode, the poor woman finally reached across me, pulled open my desk drawer, and grabbed an eraser.

My suddenly sheepish look was filled with the knowledge that what I had thought to be an early morning flirtation had only been a request for a small office supply item. 'Rubber' is an 'eraser', now isn't it?

Fortunately, I had not reacted inappropriately to her request. But from that day on I realised just how little I knew about the local language and vowed to myself that I would listen carefully to understand the real context of a discussion or question before I put my own brain and mouth in gear.

I hope that the following helps you to avoid a similarly embarrassing situation.

A

Afters – dessert, not to be confused with anything else that might come 'after' a meal such as a cup of coffee or tea. An 'after' is the sweet course following the main meal.

Arse – a person's backside, as in 'His head is up his arse.' Can also be used as a verb, e.g. 'All you did was arse around all day!'

B

Back of Beyonds – a reference to almost anything outside of Dublin or a large city or town; a country location that's not quite with it as in 'You wouldn't get me to live there. It's the back of beyonds for sure.'

Bacon – a particular cut of ham. Usually boiled to cook.

Banjaxed – broken beyond any hope of repair, as 'The car is banjaxed for sure!'

Beyond the Pale – the Pale refers to Viking times, and the area immediately surrounding Dublin and the local environs. 'Beyond the Pale' refers to anywhere outside of Dublin and is used in the modern vernacular to mean an area anywhere *other* than Dublin. The Dubs take particular delight in letting the rest of us know that we live 'beyond the pale'.

Biscuit – is a cookie. If you ask for a cookie all you'll get are blank stares.

Bird – a woman, usually a good-looking one.

Blather – as in talking nonsense, e.g. 'All she did was blather on and on.'

Blow In – a recent (like in the past 20 years) arrival in a community, e.g. 'That Richards only arrived here in '82. Don't be talking to him because he's only a blow in and will probably leave in the morning!'

Bog – while ostensibly a watery part of the Irish geography, can also refer to the toilet, as in 'Where's the bog? I'm dying to take a piss.'

Bollocking – a noun that indicates a verbal tirade as in, 'I'm going to give that fellow a bollocking when I catch him!'

Bolloxed – a noun indicating that a person is either very tired, very drunk, or both as in 'I'm bolloxed tired.'

Bonnet – an automobile's hood.

Boot – an automobile's trunk.

Bowsie – a noun or adjective used to describe an oafish or overtly dirty person: 'He's a real bowsie, that one!'

Bril – shorthand for brilliant.

Brilliant – meaning a wonderful experience, e.g. 'The play was just brilliant!'

Bubble and Squeak – an Irish dish of leftover mashed potatoes, cabbage, and a little seasoning all mixed together and fried on a pan. Wonderful!

C
Casualty – emergency room.

Cat – a negative term for something bad, as in 'This film was cat and I'd never recommend it.'

Chance Your Arm – to take a chance, often used in a negative manner, as in 'I'll chance my arm and have another drink. The Garda will never catch me out.'

Chemist – pharmacist.

Chin-wag – a discussion or chat, as in 'I met Breda at the shopping centre and we had a lovely chin-wag.'

Chipper – a fast food restaurant that serves Chips, among other greasy titbits.

Chips – French Fries. Ask for chips expecting Potato Chips and you'll be in for a surprise.

Cock – the male reproductive organ, not to be confused with a male chicken.

Cooker – the Irish term for a stove, e.g. 'Put the pot on the cooker.'

Cop – to discover or understand as in, 'I couldn't balance the bank book but then I copped the error.'

Cowboy – a dishonest businessperson, as in 'Don't trust him. He's only a cowboy!'

Craic – not to be confused with a mind-altering drug, 'Craic' means Great Fun, as in 'Let's go to the pub and have some mighty craic!'

Crisps – potato chips.

Cuppa – a cup of tea as in, 'Go on, have a cuppa. I know you want one!'

Cute – usually used in a negative context to describe a person who is being inappropriately clever as in, 'That cute hoor will never succeed. Wait 'til he falls on his arse.'

D

Deadly – a term meaning 'cool', as in 'That new coat you're wearing is deadly!'

Dense – usually a pejorative word, meaning stupid as in 'I don't know why I talk to the lad because he's so dense!'

Dickeyed Up – dressed up to the nines, e.g. 'You've dickeyed yourself up for the occasion, I see.'

Divil (as in Devil) – usually a humorous observation of a person with a rude, troublesome, or cantankerous disposition as, 'Yer Uncle Harold, now he's a real divil.'

Doing a Line – exclusively courting or dating a person, as in 'She's doing a line with Jason so keep your distance.'

Donkey's Years – a great deal of time as in 'I haven't seen you in Donkey's Years.'

Drawers – undergarments, usually of the female variety.

Drink Link – a standard 'hole in the wall', or ATM. The handiest place to get cash for a much-needed pint.

Dry Shite – an exceptionally unfunny and boring person, as in 'He's such a dry shite I don't know how his wife stands him.'

Dummy – a baby's pacifier.

E

Eat the Head Off – verbal abuse, as in 'Stop eating the head off me and calm down!'

Eejit – a true idiot, as in 'You eejit, you! Get the feck out of my gob.'

F

Fag – a cigarette, not to be confused with a person of a homosexual persuasion, as in 'Give us a packet of twenty fags.' Irish people abroad must be circumspect if standing in a New York tobacconist and ordering a pack, realising that they must do their level best to avoid using this word without attracting trouble.

Fair Play – a phrase that has absolutely nothing to do with a theatrical play, it roughly translates into 'Good for you!' as in 'You've passed your math test? Fair play to you then!'

Fanny – ummm...this does not refer to a person's posterior, but rather to that part of the female genitalia located directly opposite. Use this word only with extreme caution (by the way, this also means that the term 'Fanny Pack' is not used at all in Ireland).

Feck – the socially-acceptable version of the F-word and used whenever possible, as in: 'He's a cute fecker', or 'Would you ever feck-off!' Feck rapidly descends into the four letter common word when in heated discussions. Get used to it.

Fine Bit of Stuff – a good-looking woman, as in 'Now there's a fine bit of stuff! Wonder if she'd give us a go?'

Fiver – a five-euro note, as in 'Stop being cheap and give us a fiver.'

Flummoxed – inordinately puzzled, as in 'You've confused the shite out of me and now I'm completely flummoxed.'

Fry – an Irish breakfast (or occasionally an evening meal) often consisting of rashers, sausages, black and white pudding, fried tomatoes, fried mushrooms, toast and tea.

G
Garda Siochana – the Police. In my opinion, the Irish have one of the best police forces around. They are usually courteous and effective. You address them as 'Garda', as in 'Garda, I've lost my wallet. Can you help me?' If you encounter any problems they are always a good point of first contact.

Garden – yard. The Irish spend their summers in their back gardens here, not their back yards.

Gas Ticket – roughly translates as a person who is out of his or her mind but who also has a lot of fun, as in 'She's a gas ticket when she has a pint on her.'

Gear – clothing, usually the better stuff, as 'I see you have your party gear on.'

Gersha – Irish language slang for Young Girl, as in 'Ah, you're only a gersha and don't know a feckin' thing.'

Gob – a face or mouth, as in 'He has dirt all over his gob.'

Gobshite – a person who is worse than most idiots, as in 'You know, Pat? You're a real gobshite!'

Gosson – Irish language slang for a Young Boy, as in 'Yer only a mere Gosson and don't know a thing yet!'

Gurrier – an evil person who is always bent on wrecking everything around them: 'That young gurrier will land in prison yet.'

H
Hard Neck – a person who will try anything yet not suffer from any consequences, e.g. 'Janet will be okay. She has a hard neck and nothing will bother her.'

Header (or Head Case) – a crazy or mad individual as in: 'Mad, isn't he? A real header (head case).'

Holiday – vacation.

Hooley – a party or other wild get-together, e.g. 'We got drunk as hell. It was an incredible hooley!'

Hoor – as in 'He's a cute hoor'. Usually a pejorative expression meaning that a person will do almost anything to get what they want, usually through deceptive or manipulative means.

Hot Press – built within a house, the closet for airing clothes that often contains the hot water heater.

J

Joy, The – or Mountjoy, is Ireland's premier prison. If someone tells you that they have recently come out of The Joy, then you'd best beware.

Jumper – a common sweater.

K

Knacker – also known as a Traveller or Gypsy, this is a derogative word describing someone who belongs to the Travelling Community.

Knickers – a woman's underpants.

Knob – male genitalia.

L

Langorous – absolutely shit-faced drunk, as in 'He's languorous, so stay away from him because he's going to puke!'

Lift – an elevator.

M

Maggot – a selfish, abusive, troublesome, or unclean/uncaring person, often used as 'Stop acting the maggot!'

Messages – usually used as a noun and roughly the equivalent of 'errands', as in 'I'm going into town to pick up the messages.' This word has nothing to do with communication at all, but often alludes to the purchase of groceries or other day-to-day items.

Mickey – male genitalia, as in 'He's got the weirdest looking mickey that I've ever seen!'

Mitch – to play truant from school, as in 'He mitched school today and he's likely to get suspended.'

Mobile Phone – cell phone.

Muck – dirt, soil or mud.

Muck-in – to get involved, e.g. 'Come on, muck-in and help us get this thing finished so we can go to tea!'

Muppet – a derogatory though often humorous observation of a crazed or not-quite-together individual. Also translate as 'eejit', e.g. 'What a muppet!'

N
Nappies – diapers.

Narky – bad-tempered, e.g. 'Do you have a headache or what? Then stop being so narky would you?'

Nine-Nine-Nine (999) – the Police/Fire/Ambulance emergency number. If you're American, dial 999 (not 911)

Nixer – a small job usually done in someone's spare times and completely 'off the books,' e.g. 'If you want to make a few bob I've a nixer to be done if you don't mind building some bookcases in your spare time.'

Not the Full Shilling – a disparaging remark that means a person is incompetent or mentally deranged as in 'He's definitely not the full shilling and shouldn't be allowed anywhere near anyone.'

O
Off License – a Liquor Store.

P
Pants – lady's underwear. Not to be confused with trousers. Tell a woman that you like her pants and you might get a slap in the gob.

Path – a sidewalk. People walk on paths over here, not sidewalks.

Perishing – exceptionally cold, as in 'It's perishing outside!'

Pissdabells – dandelions. At least that's what my wife calls them.

Poteen – illegal Irish spirit, equivalent to moonshine but distilled from potatoes.

Pub Crawl – a time-honoured profession in which the drinker travels from one pub to another, finally descending to hands and knees because of the amount of drink taken.

Pudding – desserts as in, 'After dinner we have a selection of fine puddings for your culinary delight!', unless the word is associated with Breakfast or an Irish Fry in which case it will refer to a meat sausage, known as black or white pudding.

Pull – getting lucky with the opposite sex as in 'Do you think we'll pull one tonight?' meaning 'Do you think I'll have some luck picking up a woman?'

Poof – a person of the homosexual persuasion.

Q

Queer – a wonder, mystery, or used as an accolade, e.g. 'It's a queer night and I'm glad that I'm home.' Not to be confused with homosexual.

Queue – a line. That is, people form a queue over here, not a line. A line is used to define a straight edge, e.g. to draw a line.

Quid – money, usually referring to whole but unspecified amounts as in, 'Dad, can I borrow a couple of quid so that I can go out with the lads tonight?' A 'quid' in the old days could also mean one Irish pound. Today, it can mean a euro.

R

Rashers – the Irish equivalent of strips of bacon.

Ride – having sex as in, 'Come on, honey. What about a ride tonight?'

Rubber – the equivalent of 'eraser'. A rubber is not a prophylactic device but rather an instrument used to remove unwanted pencil marks.

Rubber Johnny – this is the prophylactic devise: a condom.

Runners – training or track shoes.

S

Sambo – sandwich, as in 'Do you want a sambo for lunch?'

Scuttered – drunk beyond belief; 'He's been drinking all night and is absolutely scuttered!'

Shattered – exhausted as in 'It's been a horrible day and I'm just shattered!'

Shite – the socially acceptable word for 'shit,' as in 'What a load of shite!'

Slainte – Irish for 'Cheers!' and said in a similar situation. To use this word correctly, raise your glass, say 'Slainte!' and drink!

Small One – usually refers to a single glass of Irish whiskey.

Snog – to kiss or make out, e.g. 'Mum, stop embarrassing me! All we were doing was snogging…!'"

Spuds – potatoes.

Starter – appetiser.

Stir the Shit – to tease or attempt to cause trouble, usually in an innocent way: 'Would ya stop telling everyone about how drunk I got at the party last night? All ya try to do is stir the shit.'

Strange – shy, as in 'The baby is acting strange with you.'

Surgery – a General Practitioner's doctor's office.

Sweets – translates as 'candy'. Candy is a word not used at all over here.

T

Taking the Piss – joking, as in, 'Don't get mad. I'm only taking the piss with you.'

Teatime – often refers to dinner or the evening meal. It is never used as the English use the word (e.g. a mid-morning or mid-afternoon tea).

Thick – usually meaning that a person is obstreperous, angry, or intentionally stupid, as in 'He's as thick as a plank and won't listen to anyone.'

Tinker – a derogatory word for a person of the Travelling Community but based on fact in that many Travellers were tinsmiths in days gone by.

Toilet – exactly what it means: e.g. a Men's or Women's bathroom. The Irish do not use the term Restroom. If you ask for a Restroom they'll probably think that you're looking for a place to lie down for a week or two.

Trap – mouth, as in 'Close that trap, would ya, and give me some peace!'

Travelling Community – are a native Irish minority group, set apart from the mainstream of Ireland's more settled community, and known for their nomadic way of life, and unique language and culture.

Trousers – used as a replacement for Pants, as in 'Put a belt on those trousers before they fall down around your ankles!'

Turf Accountant – a Betting Shop. A great place to put a few quid down on the horse of your choice.

W

WC (Water Closet) – the Irish *do not* use this term for the toilet or loo; my understanding is that it is a term applied only in the U.K. and other British lands.

Wellies – outdoor boots.

Y

Yoke – one of the most versatile words in the Irish vernacular, a 'yoke' can be used in place of the American 'thingamabob', e.g. 'Hand me that yoke over there!' A great word if you're suffering from a hangover and have trouble remembering anything including your own first name.

References

How to Get Here

Ireland is now served by a wonderful choice of airlines and ferries. In the old days, we had to get here via charter jet or the ubiquitous and expensive Aer Lingus daily flight from New York City. Now, things are better and prices have come down too. By the way, prices have also fallen for trips to and from the rest of Europe, making it wonderfully inexpensive to fly in from or return to the Continent. Here are just a few of the many choices:

Airlines:

Aer Aran (www.aerarann.ie) – with flights serving the U.K. This airline also serves Ireland's Aran Islands, located on the west coast of this country.

Air Canada (www.aircanada.com) – with flights to Montreal and beyond.

Air France (http://www.airfrance.ie) – flights to and from Paris and onward through France, the rest of Europe and the world.

Aer Lingus (www.aerlingus.com) – to/from the United States, with arrivals in Dublin and Shannon and departures from New York, Boston, Chicago, Washington DC, and Los Angeles; to/from Europe, check out their website for an extensive list of European destinations.

American Airlines (www.aa.com) – serving much of the United States.

British Midlands (www.britishmidland.co.uk) – for inexpensive service to and from the U.K. and beyond.

City Jet (www.cityjet.com/) – serving London City Airport and Spain.

Continental Airlines (www.continental.com) – Dublin arrivals/departures only and service to Newark, New Jersey and onward.

Czech Airlines (www.czechairlines.com/en/worldwide/ww_home.htm) – direct flights to and from Prague.

Delta Air Lines (www.deltaairlines.com) – with service to Atlanta, Georgia and onward.

Finnair (www.finnair.com) – for direct flights to Finland.

Iberia (www.iberia.com) – direct flights to Spain.

Ryanair (www.ryanair.com) – great prices to destinations all over Europe.

SAS Scandinavian Airlines (www.scandinavian.net/) – direct to Copenhagen and beyond.

Swissair (www.swiss.com) – with flights direct to/from Zurich.

US Airways (www.usair.com) – Dublin arrivals and departures only and service to Philadelphia and onward.

For more listings of airlines serving Ireland go to www.dublin-airport.com. This website will only provide you with airlines serving Dublin Airport, Ireland's main aerial terminus. However, do remember that Ireland is also served by other International Airports including Shannon Airport, Cork Airport, Galway Airport and Kerry Airport.

A Survivor's Guide to Living in Ireland

Ferries:
Irish Ferries (www.irishferries.ie) – sailings from Dublin Port and Rosslare Harbour, and transporting you to/from either Liverpool or Holyhead. Connect by bus or train to London or vice-versa.

Stena Ferries (www.ferryport.com) – as above plus sailings from Northern Ireland to the northern parts of Britain.

Staying Here
B&B's (www.irish-bnb.com)
As part of my day job I've had the pleasure of working with any number of Irish B&B's located throughout the country. The constant stream of compliments from their foreign guests is always wonderful, though unsurprising. Invariably, tourists never forget the warmth of the Irish welcome. Prices have gone up a little, but the price is worth it if only for the incredible breakfast.

Hotels:
Ireland has plenty. Some of the major hotel chains include:

Great Southern Hotels (www.gsh.ie)
Ryan Hotel Group (www.ryan-hotels.com)
Jury's Hotel Group (www.jurys.com)
Adare Manor (www.adaremanor.ie)
Renvyle House Hotel (www.renvyle.com)

Ireland also has its fair share of 'international' groups including Holiday Inns, Best Western, and similar.

Irish Citizenship
For more information on Irish Citizenship, go to:

www.justice.ie (the official website for the Irish Department of Justice, Equality and Law Reform).

www.oasis.gov.ie (search for 'Irish Citizenship').

Irish Taxes
Search the following, depending on your requirements.

Motor Tax – www.eforecourt.com/php/cartax.php
Income Tax and VAT – www.revenue.ie, then click on their
FAQ's button, and choose your poison for more
information.

Buying a House
Just like the US, Ireland has any number of Internet sites
available that are devoted to this subject. Simply go to
your favourite search engine and search 'Ireland
Property'. That said, here are a couple that I recommend:

www.sherryfitz.ie
www.gunne.ie
www.myhome.ie

Getting that Job
If you can, try to get access to a couple of the local
newspapers. They're filled with jobs especially during the
weekends:

National Newspapers:
The Irish Examiner
The Irish Independent
The Irish Times
The Sunday Business Post
The Sunday Times (Irish Edition)
The Sunday Tribune

Internet Job Sites:
www.jobs.ie
www.irishjobs.ie
www.irishtimesjobs.com
www.recruitireland.com
www.monster.ie

Starting a Business
A variety of Irish funding and support agencies are available to help would-be entrepreneurs. You might check out the following websites:

IDA (Industrial Development Authority) – www.idaireland.com

Enterprise Ireland – www.enterprise-ireland.com

Small Firms Association – www.sfa.ie

Other Useful Sites
Simply search 'Ireland' on your favourite search engine and see what comes up. Some of mine include:

www.ireland.travel.ie	For more information on B&B's and general travel.
www.beamish.ie	Take a virtual pub crawl from this old-world producer of stout.
www.guiness.com	Learn more about the history of the grand-daddy of all stouts.
www.irishcountrykitchen.ie	Real Irish recipes, and boy are they good!
www.2fm.ie	News, sports, and what's happening from this leading Irish radio broadcaster.

And if all else fails why not just climb on an airplane and find out for yourself?

Acknowledgements

In this section the author is supposed to thank all those people who helped to produce their book, no matter how large or small that contribution might be. In that I'd like to continue living here, I'd best get to it before being summarily kicked out of the country.

So to Michael Scott, friend and fellow writer, who spent any number of cruel hours reading and rereading the original manuscript, suggesting changes that were (often) completely ignored. To Liam O'Neill, fellow expatriate, who remains constantly supportive.

To Paul Tierney, brilliant graphic designer, who struggled valiantly with the cover of this book. To John Thewlis and Ultan Coogan, firm Irish friends. To Alice Raynaud, French explorer and fellow immigrant, who contributed a Continental perspective to the manuscript. To Pat Downey who let me put words in his mouth.

To Bernadette, who also read the rough draft despite deep misgivings, to ensure that I wouldn't tell too many lies. To Colette Ducie and Sarah Parke, office colleagues and bestest friends, who put up with my idiotic blathering as I slaved over these few words.

To the people of Navan, my friends and neighbours, who opened their hearts and minds to this poor Yank – no more so than on September 11th 2001 – as I fought to find my way.

And finally to my old boss at Avis Rent-a-Car who fired me back in 1982 despite the fact that I had a newly arrived daughter and a humongous house payment. If you hadn't done so I never would have made it to Ireland. You are forgiven.

Slán libh agus sin á.

(photo by Cathy Richards)

Tom Richards is a best-selling children's novelist and a produced screenwriter. He continues to live in Navan with his wife, three children and Rocky, a very large dog.

Someday he might decide to live somewhere else. But not today, thank you very much.